IF THEY SAY NO

JUST SAY Next!

24 Secrets for Going Through the Noes to Get to the Yeses

John Fuhrman

Bestselling Author of REJECT ME—I LOVE IT!

If They Say
NO
Just Say
NEXT!

JOHN FUHRMAN
rejectme@aol.com
Copyright © 2001 by John Fuhrman
ISBN 0-938716-36-0

Published by
Possibility Press
e-mail: posspress@excite.com

Other Books by *Possibility Press*

Brighten Your Day With Self-Esteem	*Are You Living Your Dream?*
No Excuse!	*Full Speed Ahead*
No Excuse! I'm Doing It	*Reject Me—I Love It!*
No Excuse! The Workbook	*The Electronic Dream*
If It Is To Be, It's Up To Me	*Focus On Your Dream*
Are You Fired Up?	*Time And Money.com*
Dream Achievers	*Dump the Debt and Get Free*
SOAR To The Top	*In Business And In Love*
Get A GRIP On Your Dream	*SCORE Your Way To Success*

Tapes by *Possibility Press*

Turning Rejection Into Direction

Manufactured in the United States of America

Dedication

This book is dedicated to the dreamers. They are the ones who create possibilities. This book is for you. It will help you stay the course. Keep dreaming. For as long as there are dreams, there is hope for an even brighter tomorrow.

CONTENTS

PART THREE   STAYING POWER

PART FOUR   SUCCESS

Acknowledgements

This book is an accumulation of credit due. Every page, thought, and word was acquired with the guidance and experience of those who have succeeded before me. Without their confidence in me, I may never have put this knowledge into book form. Thank you for believing in me and helping me stay focused on my dream.

I was able to write these pages largely because of the dedication and support of those who are driven to help others succeed. Those who provide a vision to some who may be temporarily blinded by the discouragement they feel about their current circumstances. These leaders are not only business role models, but shining examples of principled living and I am humbled to pass along their message of hope.

Thanks to those of you, who have touched my life through your written and spoken word, whom I've never met. I acknowledge you in honor of your silent mission towards success. I write these words in homage to those you've helped with hopes that they see the results of your efforts in these pages and return to thank you. In lieu of that, I'm also thanking you for them.

I salute those whose example is of focusing on others instead of themselves. Your clarity of purpose helped me through pages when the words weren't coming. Once I took my eyes off the page and looked at those I might help, balance returned, and I was able to complete my task.

I share these words with all of you with hopes you will do the same for others. This information is a gift given to me to pass on to all I can. Any talent I may have been given for putting words on paper is small in comparison to the life changing examples of your leaders. I acknowledge them and give thanks for their assistance and example.

Also, thank you God. Without you, none of this would have been possible.

"If you are unwilling to change, you have already reached your maximum potential."
John Fuhrman

INTRODUCTION

When you were a child, did you ever ask your mom for something after your dad said, "No"? I did. I always asked one parent, then the other, until I got the answer I wanted. I would then go back and inform the parent who gave me the negative response that the other one gave me approval. It was as if I thought I could change my other parent's mind. I wasn't smart enough to take the "yes" and run. I wanted to make it unanimous!

Many times it worked, but it also backfired on occasion. The parent who said, "No," would then meet with the other and explain the situation. That was when I often got in trouble. Yet, if I wanted something badly enough, it was well worth the risk. It took a special talent to pull that off. I believe most everyone has done this at some time or another. Unfortunately, it seems, that as adults, many of us have forgotten how this works.

This book is a guide to rediscovering that talent. However, I'm not training you to create conflicts with your parents again! You're going to learn (or be reminded) that one "no," from one person, is *not* the end of the world. It's not even the end of the day (unless, it's midnight, of course)! You'll learn how to apply the talent you may have once used in your "negotiations" with your parents, to the people you're now coming in contact with as an adult. When you have a goal or a dream, "no" is irrelevant. You get beyond the "no" and continue on the journey until you get the answer you need to make things happen.

It's like the old joke about the man wearing rags selling pencils on the street corner. A passerby asks, "How much are the pencils?" The man in rags replies, "One million dollars apiece." Startled, the passerby responds, "You won't sell many that way." To which the man in rags smiles and answers, "I only need to sell one!"

You're in the driver's seat of your life. The more you adopt this attitude that nothing's going to "rattle your cage," the better off you and those who depend on you will be. The theme is simple – *Don't base your life on the answers you get. Keep asking questions until you get the answers that lead you to the life you want.* When you're building the business and a prospect says "no," would you call it quits? I hope not. If you only needed a few people to make your business successful, would you let the "noes" shut you down? Or would you remember that there are over 270 million people in the United States alone, (or millions of people in whatever country you live in outside the U.S.) that you have the freedom to speak to?

There was a television commercial about a car a few years back. It starts off with kids coloring and a teacher saying how important it is to stay within the "lines" – that the lines are our friends. Then it showed an excited child with a big smile scribbling all over the page. It immediately cut away to show the child as an adult driving the vehicle off road, blazing new trails.

As far as lines go, I hope no one believes they are destined to stay within them. The lines are really the borders of mediocrity. They are NOT your friends. Do you really want to be successful? Get outside the lines, get uncomfortable, and grow! Become the person you were created to be. Find the answer that will help to put you on top of *your* world. Keep looking. The rules of life and success are one and the same. You may be living day-to-day now, but once you begin your journey of success, your life will unfold before you. Each day will be a new adventure.

I hope this book becomes a part of that journey and you see the wisdom of bringing people along to enjoy it with you. Once you begin to take the first few steps, others are likely to follow in your path as they duplicate your example. Some may even surpass what you do. Don't hold them back. Cheer them on and you'll both benefit!

"When you help enough other people get what they want, you'll get what you want."
Zig Ziglar

Part One

Starting Out

A

Chapter One

Acquiring A Taste For "No"

"Keep going until you win. After that, you'll want to go even more and win bigger than before."

"...A Hero Only Once."

That's the last part of an old, and in this case, appropriate quote. "A coward dies a thousand deaths, a hero only once." You may have heard some interpretation of this quote at one time or another, yet all the variations seem to center around one idea. Once you face and overcome potential adversity, it hurts only once. That applies whether you're skiing a "black diamond trail" for the first time, or showing the plan for the first time. If you fall down the slope or the person refuses to listen – once it happens, it's over.

The cause of anxiety for some people is that their imagination goes into "overdrive" thinking about all the negative possibilities of their situation. In the process of mentally reviewing the *imagined* peril, they scare themselves. Such people seem to focus on how many different ways there are to mess up something they're about to do. Then they mentally live out those outcomes and develop the resulting stress. Some folks even "one up" themselves when they realize they could probably survive the outcome and create a new outcome, only worse. It's truly a downward spiral and fortunately, it's avoidable!

The hero (or heroine) proceeds with the task, thinking positive possibilities rather than negative outcomes. They envision themselves feeling exhilarated as they successfully finish the ski run. They picture the new acquaintance getting as excited about the business opportunity as they are. Yet, the truth is that both the positive-thinking person and the negative-thinking person *could* experience the same negative outcome. Either one could have fallen down the slope. Both could have been flat-out rejected after they showed their marketing plan.

So, what's the difference? The one who loses "stops-in-their-tracks" because of a negative outcome. The hero however, learns, adjusts, and goes for it again. The hero continues until they reach the results they've envisioned, while the other person lives life by, "I *tried* that *once before* and it didn't work."

Another interpretation of the hero quote is one that, until now, I've kept to myself. "The thousand deaths a coward faces." I see that as the life a person without courage is sure to lead. One dead-end day after another. They develop a mental stiffness from all the finger pointing they do, blaming the world for all their problems. The amount of creativity they use to come up with the excuses, for where they are and what they're not *willing* to do, is *incredible*. What if they would use the same creativity to consider the ways they *can* do something instead of how they can't? Well, the good news is they *can* "switch gears"! As more of us focus on what we can do and go do it, all of us will have many more heroes to admire and learn from, won't we?

Hit 'em Again, Harder

You need to acquire a taste for rejection and realize the positive outcomes you can achieve by *growing through it* (not just going through it), rather than avoiding it. Attacking your challenges at full speed helps you maintain your self-esteem (the respect you *feel* for yourself). It also causes you to be more confident so you can overcome your next obstacle. Charging at adversity not only enables you to sometimes blow it away, but if you discover it's something that can't be changed, you won't let it bother you either. You'll learn to accept it and be creative in working around it to get where you want to go.

My son, John, decided he wanted to play football more than anything else in the world. For the past five years, he played soccer. Now, at the age of 11, football was to be his game. The only suggestion I gave him was, "Play for the team and give nothing less than your best."

His first mistake occurred at his first practice. He wasn't first in line for the tackling drill. Now, you may be asking, "What difference could a place in line mean in a simple drill?"

John watched the others in line before him and imagined how each collision would feel when it was his turn. He began thinking of ways to soften the blows. By the time it was his turn, he practically *walked* towards his opponent and tried to lightly push him down. The result he got was a fulfillment of his vision. He crumpled to the field in pain.

A few short weeks later, when the season started, he became the leading tackler on the team. What caused the change? His coach firmly told him to run full speed at the opponent and tackle him. When he did, the sound was almost deafening. John was the first to jump up! After a few seconds of shock, he realized that nothing hurt. His opponent was also fine, yet John had accomplished his mission and was pain free. Because he was in a situation where he had to repeat the same task over and over, he learned that *the best outcome occurs when you just go for it!* Now when the coach wants to teach the team something new, who do you suppose is at the front of the line? What about you? Where do *you* stand in the line of life?

"No" Can Take You Where You Need To Go

When you're ready for a potential "no" you're not allowing yourself to be hurt by it. You realize the "no" can't stop you from getting what you want in the long-run. In fact, it can actually help you get to your dream destination faster than a whole bunch of weak "yesses." A genuine "no" has a valid reason behind it. Their reason may be imaginary or unimportant to *you,* but the person saying "no" believes they have given the right answer for them. It's likely they have conviction and are determined to maintain their position. Otherwise they would probably have asked you a question instead of giving you a decision. If you're building a business for long-term security, don't you want people who stick to their convictions, regardless of what the rest of the world thinks? Circumstances change, you know. You may get a "yes" from some of these folks down the road.

When you take a "no" with a positive attitude, often you can be relaxed and open-minded enough to discover the reason for it. If it's a "no" because they didn't understand the plan, you can deal with it. Or they just may be going through a period where they have a "full plate" of things they need to do. Even though you may make some suggestions, they still may not budge from this position. It could be true that they're currently all-stressed-out because of certain things that are happening in their life that they need to resolve to move-on. You can then exit favorably with an openness to return when things get better. Either way you're not putting the relationship at risk in response to their "no."

"No" Is Just A Beginning

One of the people in my group, who was just starting out, had a prospect they felt would be well-suited to this business. Since this new distributor had only seen the plan once, I thought it would be a good idea for me to show it for him. As I began showing-the-plan, the prospect jumped up and glared at me, "I know exactly what this is and I'm not interested!" I was surprised at how angry she had become in an instant and asked her why she was so upset.

She explained that she had been "involved" once before and all they did was get retail customers. She told me through hard work and contacting she had developed a lot of steady customers. The trouble was, she was spending a ton of hours getting orders right, doing refunds, shipping, billing, and almost becoming a store for the neighbors. Too much work for very little return. There was absolutely no way she was going to do *that* again. I agreed with her 100%.

Once I told her that I wouldn't totally focus on retail customers either, she seemed to relax and be in a better listening mood. I began asking questions to see if there was something she might be interested in. The first thing I told her was that she never needs to directly approach people to find new customers. All she needed to do was to simply let them know that she had found a way to save time and money on virtually all the products they use every day. Then she could ask them if they'd like to save time and money too. Be sure to check with upline regarding what programs are available for getting on "the-fast-track."

Once she saw and understood the plan, and looked at her potential to be successful rather than focusing on the extra work, she got excited. She's now in my group and doing just fine.

The second example, I honestly don't want to talk about. But since I learned such a valuable lesson, I'll share it with you anyway.

I got so caught up in the possibility of this person getting in my group, I forgot to listen. I not only nearly prevented this person from getting in, I almost quit over his response. It was my dad. When he first heard I was in the business, I had to listen to all the "war" stories he had heard over the years about how much this guy "lost," or how much product that one got stuck with. You may know the routine. (I've never known anyone who has lost anything in this business.)

After a while, he noticed I was excited about the business, and my attitude about life and other things was constantly improving. I went to him, helped him build a dream, and shared some details about the business. I taught him the importance of attending functions, listening to tapes, reading the recommended books, and so on. He looked at me, asked if I was finished, and then he said, "No!" I was crushed. I felt that if this business wasn't good enough for my father, no way would it be good enough for me.

Two weeks later he had a quadruple bypass operation. Now he's healthy as a horse and in my business. He just had so much on his mind at the time, he couldn't think about next week, let alone another business.

Once you learn that *"no" is a beginning* instead of an end, you can gradually discover the reasons why certain people may not be getting "in." Some of them are scared. Others want to see what you'll do. When you acquire a taste for "no," and talk to a large number of people, the same people who once said "no" may change their mind later and join you. Don't you think that's worth it? Remember, people will only follow someone who is committed to and enthusiastic about the business and what it can do. Does that describe you?

"Success is going from failure to failure without loss of enthusiasm."
Sir Winston Churchill

L

Chapter Two

Let's Get Real

"It's worth doing whatever it takes, including going through the 'noes,' to make your dreams come true."

No, No, A Thousand Times No

"Everybody I talk to says 'no.'" This is the number one reason people give for quitting the business. When they put emphasis on getting a "yes" answer and it doesn't always happen, most people simply aren't prepared. They don't know how to handle it. They weren't ready for people to reject them. Perhaps they had been conditioned to believe that everyone would react just like they did and get "in." Maybe nobody prepared them for the possibility that some people won't want to get in.

Did you get "in" the first time you saw the plan? Many of us had to see "it" at least a couple of times and often from different people. Yet, eventually, we got "in." Say your sponsor approached you more than once before you said, "yes." Now that you're "in" and excited about your future, imagine all you'd be missing out on if they would have given up on you after you said "no" the first time! How would you feel if you were only allowed one chance to see this and your decision was final? Then somehow you'd find out what a great opportunity this is and it would be too late. Wouldn't that be a disappointment?

The response anyone gives you about whether or not they're getting "in" the business is irrelevant. Your success will be largely determined by the number of times you share it. As long as you're "plugged-into-the-system" and learning and growing – fine-tuning your skills as you go, it's likely that the missing piece is simply that you need to show the plan to more people – lots more! You will fall short of your dreams if you put a "no" limit instead of "no limit" on the number of times you're willing to be rejected. If you give up, you have reached the end of the ride. You need to "keep-on-keepin'-on" in order to achieve your goals and dreams. You can do it!

Are You "Sick-And-Tired" Of Being "Sick-And-Tired," Like Many Others?

Always remember the reason you started your business. You may have been "sick-and-tired" of being "sick-and-tired." You had the courage to make a decision to do something to create a better life for you and your family. You may have finally decided to go after all those dreams you had stuffed away, once believing you couldn't have them. Perhaps you wanted to change your financial picture. Maybe you were feeling a lack of security about the industry you're in. Or, maybe you have always wanted to be financially independent. You may want to have more time to spend with your kids before they grow up. Whatever your reasons, they are important enough for you to do something about them. Right?

When your dreams drive you to dare to do something outside your comfort zone, how is it possible, that after only a few "noes," you may be attempting to justify returning to mediocrity? With all the passion you had the day you started, how can the negative response from a person who may not be ready this instant steal your fire? How can you even *consider* letting a person who may be "comfortable" and average, control your destiny with one little two-letter word?

Don't concern yourself with the "noes" – they'll fade away. Just remember the reasons you're asking the question – your dreams and goals – and you'll do just fine. You didn't get into this business to see how many answers you could get one way or the other. *You got "in" because you had a dream.* You got "in" because something inside you started to burn and you felt that this business was the ticket to get you where you wanted to go. And the great thing about it is, you're right! It can be your ticket to achieve whatever it is you want to achieve. You've seen others do it, and you can too.

When You Want It "Bad" Enough

When you got "in," you had a reason – probably something you want very much. Perhaps, you want more time with the kids and to be able to travel more, going wherever you want for as long as you want to stay. You may want to enjoy more time fishing, golfing, horseback riding, or something else. Maybe you like the idea of having no money pressures, or just enough extra cash to provide more income than your current job so you can afford the little extras you've always wanted.

All these reasons and any others you may have are perfectly fine reasons to build this business. And I wish you well in achieving them. But what happens when a few people tell you "no"? How much effort do you put towards your dream after you've been "shot down" a number of times? It's going to happen, so you might as well have answers to those questions.

Most of us aren't ready to face a "no." I'm not telling you to enjoy it when someone isn't willing to listen. You don't have to be thrilled when they don't get "in." But, there's no good reason for letting "noes" – the answer you don't like – affect your passion for your dream.

Suppose you're prepared for the negative. When you're ready to handle it, how will that affect the dream you have inside? Your dream will live and grow even stronger when you realize that *other people's decisions have no bearing on your destiny.* Your life isn't controlled by others – unless you let them! *What really matters is that you want your dream "bad" enough.*

When you weather a thousand "noes," you can have success you've never known. Your dreams can be turned into realities, and your family can have security that will last for generations. *As crazy as it may seem, every time someone turns you down, you're getting closer to your dreams!* The time it takes to arrive at *your* destination will largely depend on how quickly you get the "noes" out of the way as you follow the system. You're like the farmer who's sifting wheat from the chaff.

You Need The Exposure

This business is built on exposure, just like any other business. The more people you show this opportunity to, the larger and more rewarding it can get. So, you might be asking, "What's that got to do with people telling you 'no'?" When you share this opportunity with others, you "expose" yourself. The people who get-in with you will watch you for leadership and example. Those who didn't get-in are likely to be watching you too, even if they won't admit it!

When you start achieving some of your dreams, the "noes" who are watching will remember what you're doing to create your success. Some will even ask you how that "thing" is going! When you tell them your efforts are responsible for the "extras" (like more time and money) you now have, they may pay attention. I can tell you, from personal experience, that as I grew, some of these people *called me* and *asked* to get "in"!

You may have some of your most committed distributors in the people who, later, contacted you to get-in. They may be very loyal and productive. They have seen the "before" and "after" in you. They have watched you grow both personally and financially. *They know this works!* They have the proof. That, along with their dreams, can keep them going for a long time as they go through the "noes" to get to the "yesses."

Some of those who refuse this opportunity may never change their minds and that's OK. That's just where they are. The benefit to seeing them again is that once they observe your attitude and determination, it's unlikely that they'll speak negatively about this business to others.

Many people "wimp-out" on themselves if they hear a few "noes." That's often because no one's prepared them for reality. The truth is, nothing's for everybody. That's OK. There's still plenty of "yesses" out there. And the great news is, when you help enough of the "yesses" to be successful, you can make your own dreams come true. Give and then you'll receive!

The question is, how far are you willing to go to live your dream? When you decide to go all the way, and take consistent action, using the tremendous system that's already in place, your chances of success are excellent. Approach the business with the attitude of, "If other people can do it, so can I. I can blast through the bumps in the road, like they did. I'll just keep my eyes on my dreams!" Think like this, and you'll win!

Remember the story about Edison and the lightbulb? He didn't invent it by quitting after a few attempts. In fact, he tested over 1,000 different things before he found the solution! Was it worth it? Look how many people benefited because he kept on! How much are you willing to do to get the results you want in *your* life? How many people are you willing to help to make *your* dreams come true?

Some naysayers may make comments like, "If it's so easy, why isn't everybody doing it?" They've missed the point. This journey is simple, but like anything worthwhile, it requires effort! *The only way to live your dream is to do what big dreamers do to make their dream a reality.* They have dogged determination. They just keep going making progress each day toward reaching their goals. This business is loaded with big dreamers – people from all walks of life who used this business as a vehicle to get where they wanted to go. They kept playing until they won. How about you? Will you keep playing until you win?

It's human nature to want things to be easy. To succeed, though, we all need to be open to challenges. Challenge yourself and you're sure to grow! The business is *simple*. Part of it's simplicity is that when you help enough other people achieve their independence, your freedom is assured. It's not always easy, but it's not always difficult either!

"This one thing I do...I press on to the mark."
Phillipians

Chapter Three

Will You Listen?

"Luck occurs when opportunity and preparedness meet. You get 'yesses' because you've prepared yourself by going through the 'noes.'"

We've All Heard It Before

Statistic after statistic. Each one worse than the one before. It seems that many people who are working for a living will now need to work many more years than they originally planned. Between putting kids through college and caring for aging parents, many of these folks can't even considering retiring. And when they do, it's sad that most people retire on two-thirds of the income they couldn't afford to live on before!

What kind of life are you headed for? Are you striving to make profits higher for your employer so that when you retire, you can take your life skills and flip burgers? That is, of course, until you can claw your way up the fast-food ladder to "fry captain."

You and I both know this isn't the first time you've heard this stuff. The goal of this book is to move you to do something about it. Something that can help you take back the control of your life. Something that will reward you for your efforts and recognize your success. Something that will provide the type of security you *thought* would be there when you first entered the workplace.

"Oh, You Get Used To It"

I grew up in New Jersey. For years, the response I got when I told people that, was either, "What exit?" or "How could you stand the smell?" The first answer was simple. I told them the number. The second reply was a resigned, "Oh, you get used to it."

Now I live in northern New England and people ask me, "How can you stand the winters?" "Oh, you get used to it," is the standard reply. When I was working long hours in the car business, I was often asked, "How can you put up with the pressure and the time away from home?" You guessed it. "Oh, you get used to it!"

Most things, even unpleasant ones, can be tolerated when you do them often enough. The first plunge into a swimming pool is usually a shock, until you *get used to it*. But soon you get comfortable – until it's time to get out, that is. Then you need to get used to the "cool" air all over again!

The same is true for this business. In all likelihood, you're going to hear "no" more often than you hear "yes." But, you'll get used to it! Unfortunately, many of us resist meeting new people because of how uncomfortable we felt when someone told us "no" in the past. One of the "secrets" of success is you just need to keep doing it, until you meet the "yesses." Many of you already are used to "noes" in other life situations. You need to be open to the possibility of being turned down more often than you'll be accepted. When you go through enough "noes," the "yesses" will come more frequently. Before too long, you'll even get used to the "yesses"! (Won't that be a treat?)

Talk To More Listeners

One of the ways to reduce the amount of "noes" you're experiencing is to approach more of *the right people*. You're probably saying to yourself, "If I knew the right people I'd already be successful."

I'm not saying to look only for people who'll say "yes" to what you're sharing. You and I both know they're impossible to spot. What I mean by *the right people*, are those who indicated they might be open to an opportunity. While they may not give you a "yes," it's likely they'll give it more serious consideration before deciding. In other words, they'll probably be more open to listening to what you have to say before they decide what they're going to do. That's the best you can hope for – to really be heard. Increase the times you're in front of such people, and your business can grow that much faster.

How do you find *the right people*? You *listen* for them. That's all. Just *listen*.

They may say, "If I earned a little more, I could pay off my credit cards." Your ears perk up. You think, "Is this one of them?" Or they could say, "To make ends meet, I spend too many hours away from my family." Your "antennas" go up. You say to yourself, "Maybe this one?" What if they say,

"There's got to be a better way"? Or, "I'd do anything if...."? Get the idea? Which one is your best potential prospect? Actually they could all be excellent candidates. There are a lot of people with "average" habits (like watching 42 hours of television a week) who are miserable but won't admit it. Why? Because then, they might need to *do something*. Heaven forbid – they may need to actually rise from the couch and *move!* Frankly, I'd love to talk to nothing but those people who are obviously dissatisfied; those who sound like they may be looking for an opportunity – a chance to make some changes in their situation.

Of course, there are no guarantees that even these people will accept what you have to share. But personally, I have a much higher success rate when I'm showing the plan to people who are at least willing to listen. Fortunately, most people are willing to listen to something when they believe it can help them solve their problems. Everyone would like some relief from the burdens they've been carrying around – like worrying about how they'll retire when they just got "downsized" and lost their pension.

You can hedge your bets even further, if you want to. When you come across someone who seems like they may be "ripe" for an opportunity, ask them this question: "Are you serious about that?" It gives them the chance to continue or simply admit they were doing nothing but complaining. If they're really serious, often they'll press you to continue. Wouldn't you feel great being pressured to share the opportunity by the person you want to share it with?

Resist the temptation to blurt out your "plan," and instead be calm, cool, and collected – ask them more questions. (They'll probably be thrilled someone is interested in their favorite subject – *them!*) Don't be anxious to get them "in." By "taking-it-away-from-them," you're posturizing, and they're likely to want it even more. It's human nature.

People often want what they don't think they can have. Remember, you want to increase your chances of success, don't you?

Ask them, "What would you do with extra time, money, freedom, and security?" Then ask what may be the most important question you could ask prior to showing anybody this opportunity – "Would you be willing to invest 10-15 hours a week for the next two-to-five years if, by doing that, you could have what you just said you wanted?" If they answer, "no," you could then ask, "How much time *would* you be willing to invest?" If they say, "It depends on what it is," or dance around the question in another way, you may not have a serious prospect, afterall. Or you may just have a person who's cautious and needs all the facts before they respond to such a question. I know of a couple who took three months to check everything out before they got-in. Their sponsor is glad he was patient because they are now his strongest leg of distribution, with a business that spans the globe.

If they don't show the least bit of interest, once you mention a potential time investment, they're probably not interested. They may turn down anything that requires "extra work." And even if they did get "in," they'd probably either quit or do nothing. You might also be tempted to "force" their success, which has results similar to trying to raise the dead!

I'm not telling you to ignore these people totally. Some of them could have a change of heart and later be valuable to your organization. They could also lead you to someone who's "hungry" and who'll work for what they want. They might want to get "in" just to use the products and services. Or they might choose to be a retail customer. However, since each situation is different, if you're not sure what to do, your best bet is to check with upline to find out what they recommend.

How Do You Sound?

Many experts have tackled the topic of listening skills. Books Like Dale Carnegie's *How To Win Friends and Influence People* and *How To Start a Conversation and Make Friends* by Don Gabor are excellent resources. I suggest that you look at what *they* have to offer as well. They can give you even more ways to truly *hear* what others are saying. For now, though, let's focus on another aspect of listening that's perhaps the most ignored – yourself! Have you listened to yourself lately?

Do your words say that you believe in this business, while your tone of voice sounds like you're unsure? Are you encouraging people to get "in" with your words, but does your heart wonder if even *you* are really "in"?

"It's not what you say, but how you say it," is an old expression that certainly applies to this business. To effectively communicate with others, you first need to honestly believe that this is the vehicle *you* are using to move-on with. When you're *truly committed*, your voice will sound like it! Once you believe in something *strongly* enough, you'll commit to doing *whatever-it-takes*. Your conviction becomes obvious in your tone of voice. This is vital to your success. Remember, success is a journey, not a destination. Your decision to solidly commit is the beginning of the journey and your success.

People, as a rule, like to associate with other successful people. They like to "get-on-a-train-that's-moving-on." Your commitment speaks louder than your words. Your belief and decision to follow this through will be what people hear, see, and feel when they're interested in moving-on themselves.

When others see that you have listened to and are following your dreams, they're more likely to want to associate with you. They'll want to *hear, see, and feel* whatever it is that's changing you. When you listen to yourself and you hear your own self-confidence, others will hear it too. You'll spark the interest of true prospects to want to hear what you have to say. That's when it'll be even more exciting to share this opportunity.

"The way to develop self-confidence is to do the thing you fear and get a record of successful experiences behind you."
William Jennings Bryan

Chapter Four

Attitude Is Everything

"We believe that developing a positive hopeful attitude is necessary to reach our goals."
Rich DeVos

It's Not Just What You Do

When you watch skilled athletes win, you're not only seeing the results of that competition. You're also seeing the outcome of the years of training it took them to get to that level of accomplishment. Some successes are measured in thousandths of a second. In less time than it takes for the blink of an eye, you can have the difference between winning and second place. It's the difference between fame and a trivia question, glory and perhaps oblivion.

The difference of a thousandth of a second can't be based solely on ability. That minuscule amount of time isn't just the result of talent, strength, or training. There's one key ingredient left. Many of us have seen it quoted in the sports pages so often, that perhaps we take it for granted. "The victor just wanted it more." So, what does that mean?

In most cases, those who are victorious mentally pictured themselves winning beforehand, while the others may have simply seen themselves in a race. Successful athletes see the finish line, instead of the long hours of practice it takes them to even make it to the race. *They focus on the results they want from their efforts, rather than the effort itself.*

Keep Your Eye On the Prize

A farmer wanted to give his land to one of his three sons. He offered each of them the same chance to win it. After a heavy snowfall, he took the boys outside and pointed to a tree about a 100 yards away. He said to them, "Whoever can walk to that tree in a straight line will get the farm."

The oldest pushed his brothers aside and boasted how he would let them work for him on his farm. Then he began carefully placing one foot in front of the other. He kept his eyes "glued" to the ground so he could watch each foot go perfectly in front of the other. When his father told him he had gone far enough, he grinned from ear-to-ear. When he looked up, he was dismayed to see that he had practically made a complete circle, almost to the spot where he had started!

Next, the second oldest began his quest. To avoid making the same mistake his older brother made, he kept a careful watch over his shoulder. He wanted to be sure he didn't look foolish too. He was determined to travel in the straightest of lines. He could hardly contain himself when the voice of his father cried out that he was finished. He was about to turn and hug the tree when he looked to his left and saw it more than 25 yards away!

The father looked at his youngest and asked if he was sure he wanted to do this. The youngster replied that when he got to the tree he would share the farm with his brothers equally. Unlike the other two, he set his gaze firmly on the tree and began walking towards it. Even when he felt himself stumble, his focus remained solidly on that tree. He grew excited as he got closer and closer to his goal. Finally, he was able to touch the tree but didn't until he turned around to see where he had been. Never had a more perfect line been walked.

That's how you need to approach your business. Focus on your destination rather than on every step of the way. Don't dwell on what happened in the past. *Your past mistakes have no bearing on your success today*, unless you allow them to affect you. However, it can benefit you to reflect on the exhilaration of a previous victory or on a lesson you learned that could help you move-on now. Reflect on it, let it go, and move-on.

Each day is a fresh new beginning. Keep focused on your goals and dreams – which is where you're headed. You know that realistically, your life, security, freedom, and happiness *do not* depend on the outcome of just one meeting. So what if they all said "No"? What did you *learn* from the experience that can help you with your next meeting? As long as you're learning, you're growing. Keep persistently focusing and growing and then, watch what happens!

People often wonder how some folks are able to build a business faster than others. There are many possible reasons, but I feel that one ingredient in all of them is the ability to stay focused on the goal. They do not dwell on the decisions of those who won't be joining them now. Instead, they keep finding and working with the ones who are interested in changing their lives. To the rest, they just say "NEXT"!

The Attitude Of Gratitude

Be excited about talking with lots of people. Your business can grow only through the exposure provided by word of mouth. And it's just your mouth in the beginning, until you start building an active organization. It's important to be thankful for the opportunity to "spread-the-word." That sense of gratitude and your desired destination need to be your focus. Keeping this in mind can speed up the growth of your organization and therefore reduce the time it takes to reach your destination.

When you're thankful for the opportunity to spread the word, the answers of those you speak to don't seem important. If you get a "no," you'll have a tendency to say "Next!" Then you'll go on to show-the-plan to many more people than you would have if you had analyzed and agonized over each result. You're more likely to keep moving and growing, getting closer and closer to your goals and dreams.

When you don't pressure people, it gives them the chance to make a quality decision for themselves, rather than just giving you a "no" to get you to go away. *You know you'll be successful, with or without them!* You're always treating them with kindness. You're patiently giving the information they need and want. You're doing the best you can. You know you're doing the right thing for *you* – you're unattached to their response. Their response is up to them – you're just doing what you feel you need to do to share the "greatest opportunity in the world" with them.

It's also possible that your attitude may allow them to change their mind (if they said "no" the first time) and contact you later – without being embarrassed. You've allowed them to get "in" on their own terms. Remember, no one likes to be "sold," but everyone likes to "buy"!

Motion Creates Emotion

You'd probably like to have a positive attitude more of the time. Right? Why not? I admit, when I have nothing but time on my hands, which isn't very often, it's easy to question what I'm doing. If you have a few setbacks and take a break, some of you probably do the same thing. Our human nature sometimes causes us to want to place the blame elsewhere to eliminate the pain of failure.

I used to think that those kinds of moods were easy to get into but difficult to get out of. Now, when I feel a little bit of despair, a touch of negative, a fear of failure, or any other negative feeling, I look to the CURE. *I do something!* Anything. Anything, that is, that puts me just a bit closer to my destination. Sometimes I even give myself a standing ovation for making it as far as I have!

Do it! Stand up right now and start clapping as loud as you can. Throw in a couple of whistles and a bunch of yells for good measure. How do you feel? Look, if you don't think you deserve a standing ovation, why would anybody else think so? I'll let you in on a little secret. Since you have taken some steps to better your life and the lives of your loved ones, I'm giving *you* a standing ovation – yea! Why not join me?

Dreambuild Regularly – Stay In Touch With Your Dream

Another way to create a better attitude is to "visit" one of your dreams. It's called dreambuilding. The dream that burned inside me the most was to be able to spend more time with my children. When I would reach a low point in my journey, I would stop what I was doing and spend some time with them. I set a definite time limit, but I would really get into whatever the kids and I were doing.

When the time was up, I always had mixed emotions. I felt better after playing but I also felt sad about leaving them. Then I would think to myself that I can have more time with them once I achieve my goals. Whenever I touched one of my dreams, I was always able to plunge back into the fray with a renewed positive attitude because it made me feel good *about* me!

If it's a new car, van, or truck for you, rent or borrow your favorite one for a day. Drive it for a few hours. Take possession of it in your mind. Drive it into your garage. Take it to your favorite restaurant, have a nice meal, and then drive it home. Have someone take a picture of you in it. If it's the one you really want, it'll be difficult to take it back. That's good! Realize you're business can enable you to purchase that vehicle, and feel your attitude change.

Food For Your 'Tude

If left alone, your attitude will whither and die. Like your body, it needs to be nourished to be healthy. Fortunately, in this business, there's also an abundance of high-quality "food" for your attitude.

Afterall, you need a balanced diet to have excellent physical health. Why not give a boost of health to your attitude on a regular basis? How about showing your friends and business associates that proper "nutrition" for your mind is a "shortcut" to success?

The great speaker and bestselling author, Charlie "Tremendous" Jones says, "The greatest difference in your life over the next five years will be in the books you read and the people you meet." Remember to feed your mind every day by reading 15 minutes or more from a positive book. I'm sure your leaders can recommend some books that will specifically meet your needs.

This serves two purposes. Learning at your own pace from some great teachers will help you grow to lead your distributors to where they want to go. This'll help you reach your goals, one by one. Secondly, relaxing with a positive book will allow you to recharge your "batteries.

Audiotapes, available as an option through the business, are also great attitude "food." Listen to them in your bathroom as you get ready for work and when you're getting ready for bed. Turn your car into a "university-on-wheels." Listen to a positive tape rather than the negative news or "get-you-nowhere" music on the radio. Walk briskly at lunch, using your portable cassette player with earphones. Invigorate your body and your mind at the same time! Listen to tapes while you do things around the house. You'll be amazed what listening to at least one positive tape a day can do for your attitude – and your business!

It's important to associate with at least one positive person every day. Maybe things at work are tense due to the potential of downsizing. Perhaps your job is so high pressure that you can barely cope with it. With the *system* of success available to you, you can listen to a positive person while you're driving to and from work. Simply insert a tape into your cassette player and press play.

The people you'll hear are especially relatable since many of them came from where you are right now! Perhaps they've experienced exactly what you're going through at this time. How much better would your attitude be after hearing the solution to a situation that's been holding you back? You'll get encouragement that can help you overcome this situation too!

Y

Chapter Five

Contrary To Popular Belief,
You'll See It When You Believe It!

*"Whatever you can think of and believe in,
you can accomplish"*

The Difference Between Sight And Vision

Is it possible to have perfect sight and no vision? Yes! It's not only possible, but it's quite likely that you'll run into more people who can plainly *see* that this can't work than you'll have people with the vision to *see* the end result – their dreams coming true through building this business.

Didn't we all have vision as kids? My vision went everywhere and changed with the season. Every summer I saw myself playing catcher for the New York Yankees. As the leaves turned in the fall, I was scoring touchdowns for the

Giants. Then, in the dead of winter, I was streaking down center ice at Madison Square Garden scoring for the New York Rangers.

I also remember the summer of 1969. The whole family was eating pizza when I saw my newest dream on our TV. When Neil Armstrong set foot on the moon that night, I asked if astronauts ate pizza. If someone would've told me that astronauts never eat pizza I could've accepted it. I was prepared to never eat another slice of my favorite meal if it meant that I could become a spaceman!

I feel fortunate to have been raised as I was. Perhaps you were taught the same solid values. My values came from my parents and teachers. You may have acquired them from others whom you respected. I can honestly say that I was never discouraged about anything I wanted to do. My father used to tell my brothers and me the same thing over and over, "I don't care what you guys decide to do with your lives. Just be the best."

Without spending a lot of time analyzing, I believe that because we were told by an authority figure to be the best, our assumption was that the best was possible. As a result, our belief in ourselves and our ability to excel was nurtured. I'm not naïve enough to believe that all parents wholeheartedly encourage their children, like mine did. Regardless, it's up to us, as adults, to discover and put ourselves in such a nourishing environment. Fortunately, the leaders in this business provide the nurturing we all need so we can start or continue believing we can do it.

You'll find enjoyment throughout your growth in this business. It'll come as a natural result because you'll be surrounded by people who feel that the best is possible for you. The difference here is, that unlike most jobs, *you* decide what's best for you. Then you can use the support system to help you get there.

As you work towards your goals and dreams, you'll undoubtedly meet people without vision. Most of them once had it but lost it along the way because it wasn't encouraged for one reason or another. Some of them may get "in" to see if you can help them rekindle it. Do all you can to help these people build their dreams. Develop a friendship and encourage them to build their dreams and make them come true with this business. Be a good example by focusing on your dreams each day through pictures and the like.

Unfortunately, some of them may not be interested in restoring their vision. They may have become bitter and feel the world owes them. If you encounter such a person, and they refuse to listen, move-on. You can only make a difference in the lives of those who want to make a change and take action.

Some people have resigned themselves to the "fact" that this is their lot in life. They're likely to resent it when somebody comes along and suggests that their "rut" isn't as comfortable as they've fooled themselves into believing. They're probably too busy blaming others to realize that *they* are responsible for their life situation. By admitting that, they'd also be acknowledging the fact that they're the ones who need to take action. They need to get out of their "victim mentality" so they can create the life they want – that is if they're serious about moving-on. Remember, just because someone complains, doesn't necessarily mean they'll do anything to change their situation. Some people just like the attention they get when they complain.

When It's Crystal Clear, It's "Reality"

Growth requires discomfort, and sometimes it even causes pain. It's just like an exercise program. The more you want to improve, the more discomfort or pain you're likely to experience. Similarly, working toward the next level in this business, you may feel somewhat uncomfortable. Anytime you stretch, you leave your comfort zone. That discomfort, handled properly, creates a gem (your goals) from a grain of sand (your discomfort).

Now picture a perfect pearl. If it wasn't for the discomfort felt by the oyster, that pearl wouldn't exist! If the oyster could be certain of avoiding any discomfort in life, the best it could hope for is front row center, in the ice at a raw bar.

The reason you may be uncomfortable in a new situation is because of a lack of clarity. You're being faced with the unknown and you may not yet understand quite what to do. That's OK – it's just part of the process. You decide to take on the challenge of this opportunity to achieve financial freedom, which paints your destination with a broad brush. Your success is in the journey, not the destination.

It's similar to deciding you'd really like to vacation somewhere in the Western Hemisphere, but you're not sure of the exact location. "Somewhere" would be difficult to enjoy; but ultimately you do want a vacation. As you got closer to the time to go, you were able to sort out the details – compare destinations and narrow it down to a few. You could gradually see more clearly which location had the features that would give you the most pleasure. Then, as the date to reward yourself with the vacation is almost here, you decide exactly where you'd like to go this time – Hawaii.

Building this business is similar to the previous example. In the beginning, you often concentrate on *leaving* something – usually a job. As you grow, you gain a different perspective. When you begin to see that achieving your goals *is* possible – that you really *can* do it, you're likely to change your focus.

As you discover that setting goals and working *towards* them is far more rewarding than just running *away* from a job, or anything else for that matter, you'll begin to help others to change their focus, too. Run towards the positive rather than away from the negative. *You get what you focus on!* Once you begin to make your goals a reality, the proof is now *in you*. The "noes'" along the way no longer have the same negative affect as they might have had before. Instead of a negative anchor keeping you stuck to your job, each "no" becomes one more step on your way to freedom.

As you take each step, you'll become more-and-more focused. Your dreams of freedom will get very specific. You'll begin to approximate the date it will occur and you'll start making a list of who you'll want at your "retirement" party. You're likely to see this opportunity as your tool to help yourself and others grow and you'll envision yourself as a leader in the business. You'll be in the process of creating a major win-win situation.

When this shift in your focus occurs, your clearer vision helps you deal with the negative responses. You finally realize that each one brings you closer to the destination you desire. You'll get to the point where each prospect's response is irrelevant. You'll just want to share this business with as many people as possible, and let the "law of large numbers" take its course and work its "magic"!

Let's Do It Fast

Would you build this business if your success was guaranteed after you had 1,000 "noes"? Many of you would *say* "yes" but would you *actually* do it? If the results could be guaranteed, the same percentage of people would still succeed. Why? Speed? Some of the people move through their prospects more quickly. They're also very focused in the direction they want to go.

Here's what I mean. Many of us tend to dwell on a negative response far too long. If a prospect says "no" to our plan, some of us feel as if we were wounded in battle! We may leave the "front" to get to a bed, curl up, and recover from our "trauma." As our wounds heal, we have time to agonize over every aspect of the "battle" that led up to our being "wounded." It's important that you don't dwell on the wound or feel sorry for yourself. If you throw a "pity party," nobody will show up anyway! *The best way to heal quickly is to take whatever you've learned from your experience, and go for it again as soon as possible – full speed ahead!*

What you may not be aware of is this approach also applies to positive answers! Sometimes you may be so overjoyed to finally get a "yes," that you want to savor the moment for as long as possible. You may tend to hover around this person until they can't "breathe." Then you probably don't understand why they aren't building the business!

They are likely to be feeling pressured by your constant attention. They may begin to feel as if your future depends on how big they build their business. That's a lot of responsibility to deal with, especially when someone is brand new and doesn't know much about the business. As a result, their involvement may be short-lived. Some of them may even have a negative attitude toward you if they feel the only reason you sponsored them was so they could make you rich. Always remember why they got "in" this business in the first place. They may have been "sick-and-tired" of working (at their job) just to make someone else (their boss) rich. And most people don't want another job!

S

Chapter Six

Setting Higher Standards
*"To improve your game, always play with people
more skilled than you are."*

Two Ways To The Top

Some people believe that the definition of "best" is to do better than everyone else. While that may sound good here's what happens if you use that interpretation in this business.

If you show the plan to people who are less ambitious than you, aren't as much of a dreamer as you, aren't as good at meeting people as you, and aren't as serious about moving-on as you, and they get "in," it's called sponsoring "down." You know what happens should these folks sponsor anyone at all? They're likely to sponsor down too! You'll be the best in your group alright. But is that what you really want?

The other way to the top is a little more challenging, but can be many times more rewarding.

When you focus on showing this business to people who are at your ambition level and above, you're much more likely to become successful. Focus your attention on making sure that those who get into the business with you get everything out of it they can. This approach can practically push you to the top by the success you help them create. In the process, you can become an even stronger leader.

It's almost as if you sit upon the shoulders of those you sponsor. In front of you lies a grand stairway. If each of those steps up represents a goal or dream to one of your people, helping them achieve it moves them up the staircase. And as they progress, so do you! The difference between being the "best" and this scenario is that because of your efforts in helping them, you're carried up to the top as well. As you help your distributors to make their goals and dreams a reality, your goals and dreams unfold into existence in *your* life, too.

Both seem to end with the same result, you on top. Which top do you want? It's just a choice away. *Remember this – You can't help others without thereby helping yourself. And, the greatest leader is the servant of all!*

Leaders Are Found In Every Occupation

You may feel torn. You want to succeed quickly and you're willing to help others. So you may figure the best way to do that is to sponsor people who are already successful. But you may believe there are a limited number of successful people to talk to. Is that true for you? If you're equating successful with professional position (doctors, lawyers, accountants, etc.), then you'd be correct. But, that doesn't automatically mean they're leaders.

Have you ever dealt with so-called "professional" people who are so difficult to communicate with and who gave you such poor service that you vowed *never* to return to them? Is it possible these particular people aren't very good with people? Just because someone has a professional label, doesn't automatically mean they're successful or have leadership qualities. By the same token, have you ever raved about the service and attention you've received from a true professional? These examples apply regardless of whether we're talking about the other categories of professionals mentioned or a hair stylist, landscaper, mechanic, carpenter, or any other person who offers a service you may need. The point is, leaders are found in all occupations.

There are people who are skillful and know how to deal with people as well as those who don't, in any field. Some of these people also have leadership qualities which are developed or undeveloped. No matter what occupation your prospect is in, they could have the ability to relate with people as well as leadership potential. We're not talking about technical occupational skill here.

Your business is likely to grow the fastest when you find and sponsor people who are serious about using this business to substantially increase their income. Then you can "plug-them-into-the-system" so they can develop as leaders in the business. Some of these people are easy to find while most need to be diligently sought after like diamonds in an old mine. You "dig" for these "diamonds" by *talking to lots of people until you find them.* They're out there. You've seen them in your upline and in other organizations crossline. These people weren't successful distributors when they were born! Someone had to "dig" for these leaders until they found them. Some of them came into the business with mostly undeveloped potential and grew by following the system because they had a burning desire.

The question you want to ask yourself isn't, "Do leaders exist?" but rather, "Am I going to do whatever it takes to find them and help them become successful?" Then you can be the "best" *with them* as you enjoy the fruits of financial freedom together.

Read the Label

Unfortunately, many of us still place labels on each other. Since most people haven't grown past that, perhaps you can use it as a positive. What if someone were to read your "label" – what would they see? What if they wanted to read it before they got "in" this business with you? Would they be encouraged or not?

I believe we'd all like to have labels listing the finest ingredients. For those of us who aren't quite there yet, we can grow towards that end. When you build this business, though, keep in mind that having a few flaws may attract more people than perfect "packaging."

Some of you may feel puzzled about showing someone this business. In your heart you're very excited about the opportunity to make your dreams come true. But in your mind, you may be concerned that you won't explain it perfectly enough so people will understand how simple it is. Otherwise, you figure they may not be interested, thinking it's too complicated. Some of you have even used the false "logic" of putting off showing-the-plan until you get "comfortable" doing it. However, the only way you can get good at anything is to *just go do it!*

Are you labeling yourself as a "failure"? Let's change the perceived "label" to read, *willing to risk failure* rather than "failure." Successful people say, "We fail our way to success." Be willing to stand up in front of one or more people, explain this business as best you can, based on the guidance of your upline, and let your prospects form their own opinions. I've seen more success doing it that way than in any "perfect" plan. Here's why.

Your Best Is Good Enough

If you're nervous and unsure of yourself, that's OK. A lot of people are. Be sincere, do your best, and count on your organization to be there for you. Regardless of any discomfort and lack of experience you may have at showing the plan, be willing to risk potential failure. With an attitude like that, it's likely you'll become more attractive to your prospects who probably feel a bit uncertain, too.

Remember, no matter how little you may think you know about the business, chances are your prospects know even less! They may have been waiting to see, in more detail, what you've been talking about. They may believe this could be exactly what they've been looking for, but aren't quite sure they can do it, either. Your strength and courage and willingness to make some mistakes, as you focus on them and how you can help them, can give them the hope they need to take the next step.

The best you can give to your prospects and distributors, is to set an example for them to follow. Besides, when you go out night after night and show-the-plan, putting your fears aside, knowing full well that sometimes you'll be more successful than others, your personal growth will be tremendous. And as you develop as a leader, you can help others in your group become leaders as well. Through *duplication-of-the-system,* you can build a strong organization and make your goals and dreams a reality!

"Striving for perfection is the greatest stopper there is. You'll be afraid you can't achieve it…. It's your excuse to yourself for not doing anything. Instead, strive for excellence, doing your best."
Sir Laurence Olivier

Part Two

Shaping Up

G

Chapter Seven

"Ground Zero"
"Life isn't a dress rehearsal. This is it!"

Where Do I Start?

Many of you reading this have already decided that this business is the way for you to create a more secure and prosperous life. You may have even attended a few seminars, listened to tapes, and read the recommended books. While this is all excellent and it's important to continue doing these things, some of you may still have questions about how to get going.

Someone (or a couple) sponsored you into this business. Whether you got "in" because you liked their personality, the numbers excited you, or even the fact that it was the first opportunity that looked good, is no longer important; you're "in." Now, how about building the business to achieve what you had in mind when you signed the application?

Whether you've been "in" for years, or the ink is still wet on the application, get a piece of paper and a pen. Write down exactly why you signed the application in the first place. If you don't remember, that's OK. Hang in there and you'll have the fun of discovering things about yourself you may not have been aware of.

If you've been in the business a while, ask yourself, "Have I accomplished what I set out to do?" If your answer is "yes," that's terrific. Now it's time to build your dreams even bigger! If your answer is "no," perhaps refocusing on what you want will enable you to see that you are closer to your dreams than you may have realized. For example, it's often helpful to ask yourself, "Am I better off now than I was last year at this time?" Give yourself the credit you deserve!

What Could Be Missing?

Everyone who's serious about moving-on needs to set priorities and focus as they do whatever-it-takes to achieve them. But, if you've been "in" a while and you haven't progressed very far in achieving those things you originally said you wanted, you may be missing an important ingredient. It could be the catalyst you need for explosive growth.

Think. Did you get "in" mostly because you were excited about your sponsor's confidence, dreams, and attitude? That's OK. But now *you're* in the driver's seat. To build a big business, you need to appreciate, but not rely on, your sponsor's confidence, dreams, and attitude to "carry you" as you sponsor others. Your prospects and distributors will be looking to *you* to help them develop the burn to build this business! You need to be a role model who is fired up and moving in the direction of your dreams. You may be asking, "So, what do I need to do?

The first thing you need to do is think about *why* you got "in" in the first place. Sit down, review your expectations, and *"sponsor yourself."* The reason for doing this is so you're not only "in" the business but the business is also "in" *you* – in your heart, that is! Once you do that, your attitude and confidence takes over. You'll be able to help those whose reasons for "looking" are hidden deep inside them. The real benefit, though, to self-sponsorship is that it helps to immunize you against the rejection of others.

If you remain sponsored by someone else's enthusiasm, and don't develop your own, how do you expect to be able to get others excited about the business? However, when you "sponsor yourself," you've taken charge. You can then handle all the criticism from the *average-thinking people* who love to see others lull around in mediocrity. Remember, misery loves company! You become your own motivator and any outside motivation will only make you stronger.

The best way to overcome any objection is to first overcome your own. Once you totally believe in your dream and the power of the system, others will start believing you! Your enthusiasm and conviction can win them over.

How Can You Change Your Life In Only Minutes?

I'm going to ask you to do this next part on faith alone. When you do, I believe you'll see amazing results. You're going to set goals like you've never done before. You may be saying to yourself, "Not that goal stuff again." Think about it. Since successful people talk about goal setting over-and-over, perhaps there's something to it. Look where they are and then look where you are. If you see them and wish you could change places, get out a pen and a piece of paper.

What you are about to read is probably different than anything you've ever been told about setting goals. Many of you who have heard the "goal speech" before, remember being told to set realistic and attainable goals. Unfortunately, that often keeps you from driving toward what you *really* want.

Ask yourself, "Was landing on the moon a realistic goal?" "Was finding cures for polio and other diseases realistic?" How about skyscrapers, jets, submarines, Olympic gold medals, or any other accomplishments? Were any of those, or thousands of other things that make your life better, realistic? Then, if you were to go for great success like those who accomplished the preceding did, why would you set a single "realistic" goal? *Realistic is whatever you believe!*

Open your mind. Set aside 20 minutes tonight before you go to bed. Take a few pieces of paper and a pen and write 101 of the most outrageous goals your mind can come up with. Don't concern yourself with any details. Just keep on writing. When you clear your mind and focus on what you want, you'll surprise yourself with what you come up with.

Keep the list handy and review it often. Whenever you are deciding whether or not to do something, take out the list, read it, and ask yourself, "Will doing this bring me closer to any of my goals?" Once you determine whether or not doing something will help you reach your goals, your decision becomes easier. Will taking that action keep you on-track or take you off-track?

Super "Side Effects"

As you review your goals and dreams on a regular basis, you'll begin to change your thinking and doing. You'll start to see the person you'll become as you achieve these goals. When you continue doing this, you'll find that you begin becoming that person along the way toward achieving the goals. From here, it'll be more obvious that your goals and dreams are happening because of who you've become. You've got to "be" to "do" to "have." And following the system is key to this growth process. *The difference between what you are and what you want to be is what you do!*

The most positive "side effect" is the transition between how you respond to "noes" you're getting now and how you'll respond as you become more focused on the results you want. When you become more sharply focused on achieving your desired outcomes, the bumps along the journey soften and some of them eventually disappear as you learn how to anticipate and avoid certain situations. When you stay clearly focused on your destination, things like people saying "no" become less relevant to your success. You know that the "yesses" are out there and you persist until you find them.

You need a solid list of goals at the beginning of your journey, to increase your likelihood of success. Without sincerely-set goals you're like a ship without a rudder, with no firm sense of direction, bouncing around "to-and-fro." Without goals, your opinion sways with the wind. If someone says that what you're doing won't work, you may tend to agree. If a few people reject your plan, you might become hesitant about presenting it to other people. You may begin the search for the "sure thing." You might only approach those you believe are "guaranteed" to say "yes."

But what if a lot of those "guaranteed" "yesses" decided that this isn't for them – then what? If the very people you were absolutely certain you could count on passed on this opportunity, how could you ever hope to achieve your goals?

Let's take a look at the "noes" you may have gotten in the past from a different perspective. Just suppose you were mistaken about the people you were sure would get "in" and build the business. Since you were incorrect there, isn't it possible that you're also mistaken about the people you think *won't* be interested? Have you ever noticed that, with some things, it's pretty difficult to predict what people will do?

Prejudging Doesn't Work

Case in point. I had a list of people I knew and, contrary to the good advice I had received from my upline *not to prejudge people*, I divided the list into two parts. There were those I was sure would be interested and those who wouldn't. I think I kept all the names in case someone asked to see my list so I could show them how big it was!

I was amazed at how many people who I thought could really benefit from this business said they were "doing OK" and didn't need me or the opportunity. I learned later that this is often a defensive response because they don't want to admit they're really *not* "doing OK." As this happened more often, I began to doubt the business. These people pointed to my "successes" in other areas of my life and began to tell me I didn't need this. I almost believed them. I began to doubt myself and my association with this business.

One night I answered the phone and was very surprised by the conversation. The person on the line was someone I had known for a number of years. He was very successful in his current position, had a great family, lovely home, and all the other trappings of success. He was also on my "wouldn't-be-interested" list. He stated that he had heard through the grapevine that I was in the business and wanted to know if it was true.

I was very tempted to tell him that I was "in" at one time but had moved-on. I'm glad I didn't. He told me he had noticed a change in my attitude and how I had been spending more time with my family. He had shared this with his wife and she insisted that he contact me about getting "in." *He contacted me!* I didn't think it was supposed to work that way. I almost found myself questioning his logic since I had him on my "wouldn't-be-interested" list.

He explained that as he worked hard at his job and became more successful, it seemed that more and more was expected of him. His income continued to rise, but his time began to be consumed by the job. The very people he wanted to provide for, his family, missed him a lot as he worked longer and longer hours. The income was becoming less important. He needed to develop something else that would allow him to spend more time with his family.

I began to realize that, *in many cases, you simply can't tell who needs the business or the reasons why.* Since that's true, there's no need to divide your list and spend even one second of your time trying to figure out who's going to be interested and who's not. The only way to be certain is to ask everyone directly. Ask, ask, ask,…and ask some more!

"With ordinary talent and extraordinary perseverance, all things are attainable."
Sir Thomas Foxwell Buxton

E

Chapter Eight

Easy "Yesses" Produce Little Successes

"If you don't have any challenges, you won't have much success."

Treat Each Person As An Individual, Be Sensitive To their Needs, And Be Flexible

If you were to open up a store of some kind, how would you handle your first *potential* customer? Would you insist that they look at and listen to a description of every item in the store? Would you treat them as if they're less important if they didn't promise their undying loyalty to your place of business? Or, would you help them select what they came in for in a friendly, helpful manner?

You are building a business. The fact that there's no storefront, since your business is operated from your home, is irrelevant. Your "customers" are your prospects, your distributors, and also anyone else you serve who prefers to just purchase products and services from you without getting "in." Your success and growth depends on meeting these people's needs in a manner they find acceptable. Helping them to be satisfied and wanting to continue their relationship with you is far better than trying to force them to do anything.

One of the unique qualities of this business is that your distributor-"customers" are also in training to build their own business. They will tend to duplicate your attitude and what you do. Be sure to set a good example and do the right things.

Did you try to teach them too much at one time? Or did you gradually introduce them to what they need to learn so they could gain confidence along the way? As long as you're sensitive to their needs and commit yourself to helping them, whatever that takes, you can have a true win-win situation.

For example, say someone wants to work with you but first they insist they want to read the product literature and try some of the products – let them! *Be flexible* – everybody's different and has different needs. As Dale Carnegie says in *How To Win Friends And Influence People,* "A man convinced against his will is of the same opinion still." As their confidence in the products grows, you can share some business-building information when the time is right. This type of person may take a while to develop, but such people can become extremely loyal as they learn to follow-the-system.

Others may want to dive-right-in and build-it-fast. If you were using a "cookie-cutter-approach," treating everyone the same, you wouldn't have time for the person who really wanted to go. You'd be too busy force-feeding somebody who would rather go slow. You want to treat each person according to their level of development and what they want to accomplish in the business. Find out what they really want to do and help them do it! If they want to go slow, don't push, or you'll probably "blow" them out of the business.

Be A Point Of Reference Not A Finger Pointer

Paint your business with a broad brush. Allowing for diversity among those you sponsor shows others the benefits of encouraging people at all levels of interest to participate to the degree they want to do so. This process is much easier to duplicate, because people's needs and wants vary, and it fosters growth. The world is full of people who can benefit from this business. Focus on helping those who want help. Teach your distributors that an organization is a mix of individuals. When you focus on helping others, taking your eyes off yourself, you can build a strong organization and begin realizing your goals and dreams.

You probably know someone who'll do the business just because you're doing it. They have enough confidence in you to figure that if it's good enough for you, it's good enough for them. These could be the first people you share the business with. You could experience some initial success with them. If you're new, they'll understand and forgive your lack of knowledge and experience in the business. They may even point out areas where you may want to improve, because of your relationship.

When this occurs, ask them who they know on their list who would trust them enough to look at the business. This way you're covering all the bases. You're proving to your friend that the business can be built, you're helping them by working in depth (under them), and you're demonstrating the power of duplication.

It Takes All Kinds

When you open your eyes to all the possibilities, it's amazing what you'll see. The narrow focus of looking only for those who you believe will build a huge group generally doesn't work. If you agree with the old adage, "You can't judge a book by its cover," then you'll understand how limiting it is to your growth to look only for those with a good "cover."

These people often "look good, smell good, and sound great" but may let you down. Even if you're good at spotting real "catches," there are only a few of them who seem like they were born to do this. Say you find them, then what? Consider these suggestions and possibilities.

Some of the "good lookers" may be nothing more than that and consequently, you're wasting your time and effort. The other side of the coin is that some of the slow starters, when allowed and encouraged to develop, can become the most successful and loyal system followers. *By not limiting yourself to the type of person you want to sponsor, you open your eyes to the possibilities of tremendous growth.* Another benefit is that when you've helped several small businesses flourish, you not only grow but strengthen and stabilize your organization.

Besides, there will be more people who are interested and willing to work initially on a small scale than there will be big achievers. That's not to say that those who start slow won't develop large organizations, but there are people who feel more comfortable gradually increasing their income. In the process, they can grow a solid organization.

Diversify Your Business By Sponsoring Different Types Of People

Many people get into this business to diversify their income. They may want to add to what they're currently earning so they're prepared for unexpected financial difficulties. They may also want to get out of debt, and have extra money to spend on fun things. Some are serious about retiring from their job or selling their conventional business which consumes too much of their time and energy. Some may also have a big dream and see this as the way to make it happen. What are your reasons?

Sponsor a broad spectrum of people to diversify your income. Your earnings will be based on the habits of many. For example, you may have a couple of distributors who are inactive for whatever reason for a period of time. When you have lots of people in your organization, there'll be others who are active during that period. If someone quits, you still have plenty of people left. (You'll probably notice that people who quit generally weren't doing much in the business anyway!)

When you sponsor many types of people with various growth patterns, you're actually stabilizing your business. You're likely to have more excitement. You're also likely to have more people emerge as leaders who are more independent and can train others who come into the group in their respective organizations. Remember, you're not in this business to do everything for everybody in your group. *You need to encourage duplication, otherwise you just have another job!*

You only work with those distributors in your group who want help. These folks are more likely to be teachable because they've reached the point where they want to move-on. They're more inclined to be receptive to you because it's on their terms, not because they're being forced to do something they're not ready to do.

It's key that you make yourself available as well as promoting any support material offered by your upline. By doing this you're doing your best to assure that no one feels left out. They can become more active when the time is right for them. As your groups develop, you'll find you're using your time for leadership activities as you develop leaders in your organization who can carry on training in their own groups.

One of the biggest benefits of using the system to duplicate your efforts is that you aren't relying on the activity of just one distributor. If you do depend on one person to produce, you'd be creating the same dilemma that may have caused you to look at this business in the first place. When only one person controls your income, you're giving them the power to determine your lifestyle. With such a ceiling on your income, you can only do so much of what you want to do. That sounds like a *job*, doesn't it?

"The most important single ingredient in the formula of success is knowing how to get along with people."
Theodore Roosevelt

T

Chapter Nine

Tell Them, Show Them, Let Them, Compliment Them

"Time and money spent helping men to do more for themselves is far better than mere giving."
Henry Ford

Be Patient With Yourself As You Learn

For some reason people often act differently once they're in the business. They're brand new and yet they expect themselves to do the business as if they've been at it for a long time. They seem to forget what it was like when they learned how to ride a bicycle. It appears as if they can't remember what it was like the first time they were given a book to read out loud. Their mind doesn't acknowledge how it was their first day on a new job.

If I asked you to remember any of those times and how to describe what went on, you could probably go into great detail. You would talk about how hard it may have been to pronounce all the words and understand the book's message. You might remember how many times you fell off your bike before you could ride it all the way to school, or how long you were in training at work before you could be left alone to do the job.

Now hopefully you've remembered at least some of those beginning experiences. Why is it that, when you got "in" the business and you believed how big it could be for you, you may have even thought that you could be an instant success? I'm not saying that you may have thought you'd be wealthy right away. But did you think, as many new distributors do, that you "should" be "perfect" at it right from the start? Did it look simple when the people who taught you the business showed you how to do the basics? Well, it is simple. But it still takes practice to get good. Remember, these people probably have experience, and it's likely they stumbled too as they were first learning what to do.

Be encouraged and patient with yourself as you do what you're being taught to do to make this business happen for you and your family. It's important to encourage others as well as you're bringing new people into the business. Anyone who's been active in the business has stories to tell of how they messed up in the beginning and still make mistakes in the business. Why? Because we are all human and we all do the best we can. It's that simple! Those that win keep persisting – "picking-themselves-up-and-dusting-themselves-off," doing what they need to do over-and-over again until they reach their goals. Then they go after a new dream!

We Teach What We Need To Learn Most

How can you teach new distributors how to build a big business, when you're so new at it yourself? There are several optional resources you can take advantage of that can help you and your group develop. There are leaders in your upline with the experience to guide you and your group so you can have solid growth. You also have seminars and rallies so you and your people can learn current business-building techniques.

Tapes are available that can help you learn new skills and stay motivated. Your upline can suggest some tapes that would be useful to you and your group. You can also ask your upline to recommend some books that'll help you all develop in key areas. The best way to retain new knowledge is to teach it to the people you're working with who are teachable like you and eager to learn as much as they can too. *The more you promote these continuing education resources, the faster you can grow.*

Teaching others helps you focus on the new information, making it easier for you to understand and remember it. It also gets the information into the hands of your group faster. If you wait until you're an expert at the information you've received, it could be a while before your group ever sees or hears it. For example, say you just listened to a tape which explains how to blast through your obstacles. What would be better – just you learning and using the information or sharing the ideas and promoting the tape to your group? What do you believe would be the best approach to encourage growth and duplication of the system? Sharing and promoting, of course.

Tell Them First

When you learn something new from your upline Direct, spread the word quickly if it's appropriate to do so. Someone in your group may have been waiting for just that piece of information to create tremendous growth in their business. Since that's a possibility, why would you wait?

You also find out who may be challenged by this new information. Perhaps they just don't understand it. When that happens, and you need help, you can get them together with someone in your upline. Let them learn from someone who's already blazed a trail.

It's Show Time

One of the best ways to get your group involved is to have them see you in action. Regardless of the results, they can benefit from what you do.

Let's say you learned a great contacting technique from your upline. One way to demonstrate it is to get together with a few of your distributors so they can observe you using this contacting approach with people you meet. Each time you're successful, they'll see that the technique can work and they'll gain confidence in the method. However, if you goof up and lose the contact, they can learn an even more valuable lesson – that you're always doing things and it's OK to make a mistake. Be sure to keep your positive attitude and have fun with it, regardless of what happens!

Once you've made light of your mistake, quickly review the procedure and immediately try it again. This shows your people that you believe in the system and that you're committed to making what you've learned work. It also teaches them, by your example, how to respond if they don't get the results they want on the first few attempts. You'll be teaching them not to take themselves too seriously, and that in order to succeed, they must be willing to fail.

The next way to show them is to have them get a prospect who's excited and wants to learn more about how to meet people. Or find someone who just got "in" their group, and demonstrate the technique for them. This could help their group grow, which means growth for you. Duplication can occur twice since the person in your group as well as the new person (who may not be "in" yet) sees the technique. It could spur one or both of them to take their business to the next level.

Here's an important thing to remember: You also need to be teaching your people *not to try anything new,* outside of what the system teaches. Tell them to *check with their upline first* to see if it's duplicatable and compatible with the system.

Let Them Go And Let Them Grow

It's action time! You've explained some of the things you've learned and shared continuing education resources that can teach your distributors what they need to know. You've even taken the time to show them that the contacting technique that upline taught you works and can help them build a big business. Now you need to see if they've been listening and whether they'll use what they've learned. Will they keep working at their skills until they feel confident doing the business on their own? It's time to reverse roles.

Let them show *you* what they've learned. Have them use the technique you've taught them with a real prospect, as you observe. It's essential for everyone involved to understand, at this point, that results aren't the important part of this exercise. The exercise is the main focus – *learning by doing* is an indispensable part of success training. People only learn so much by gaining a general understanding of what to do – *action is key!* People who are serious about achieving their goals and dreams *take action.* All the talk in the world won't make up for inaction. We all need to "walk-the-talk," instead of just "talking-the-talk." Aristotle once noted that, "The quality of life is determined by its activities."

You can invest some time discussing how the contacting exercise went and what, if anything, the distributor could have done differently to get a better result. No matter what happened, though, the outcome isn't as important as the doing.

You'll Have Plenty Of Positives To Talk About

Regardless of the results of the exercise, there's lots of things you can compliment them about. The first thing you can compliment them on is the fact that *they did it – they took action.* Great! What a breakthrough! On faith alone, they proceeded with something new and unfamiliar. That takes courage. You can let them know that this is the first step towards success in anything. And as Dr. Robert Schuller says, "Beginning is half done"! "Shifting gears" and moving out of our "comfort zone" is how we succeed and gain momentum in the direction of our dreams and goals!

Second, you can tell them how well they did with certain aspects of the contact, or the entire contact (whatever's true) for their first time, and that they'll just get better-and-better at it with practice. Assure them it gets easier and easier each time they do it. Here's where they learn that success comes by doing, regardless of the results. You can tell them that even the most experienced distributors don't always get "yesses" – they get lots of "noes," too.

The last thing you need to be ready to talk about is in the event they experience a massive flop. Since you're there to "pick-them-up, dust-them- off, and point-them-in-the-right-direction," they are less likely to listen to someone who told them this won't work. You need to remind them of all the successes they have had to this point, including the brave decision to take control of their own life. (If they don't have a history of successes, share a true story of something you or someone else did while contacting that led to a "disaster." They need to learn to laugh at themselves and know they're not alone.)

Teach Them How To Handle The "Noes"

You also need to let them know that the person who said "no" may have several negative situations hanging over them that they need to work through before their mind is free to tackle anything new. The timing may not be right for them; like when I showed this to my dad two weeks before his by-pass surgery. It just wasn't a good time. Once he was back on his feet though, *he came to me!*

Let them know one of the main keys to success is to be *persistent* – get the "noes" out of the way so you can get to the "yesses." If they let just one "no" stop their progress, they'll never know how good it can be to reach one goal and dream after another.

There's one question you need to consider for yourself, as well as for all those in your group – "Where is the power?" If you or someone you know lets a rejection stop their progress, the word "no" now controls them. If given such dream-stealing power, that little word can create a fear that can blind and paralyze us. Like anything else, the longer you focus on it, the more power you're giving it. You need to change your focus – just say "NEXT!" to yourself and focus on your dreams and on helping those who want your help.

By the time you were 18, you probably heard the word "no" over 150,000 times; yet you're still alive! That tells me that the word itself is virtually harmless. Yet where does its power come from? People have *given* it power through their fearful response to it! That fear (negative energy) magnifies its power. The fear is what can really grow, if allowed to. As you continue to go forward in faith, knowing that there will always be "noes" in life – that everyone gets them, you can learn to accept the "noes" as just a part of the process. You know you're moving-on and you're finding the "yesses" who'll be moving-on with you. Haven't *you* said "no" to others before? Sure you have! We all have even if it wasn't direct or was covered-up by our inaction. You've probably given others the opportunity to say "Next!" Now it's your turn!

Negative outcomes are only important in the sense that they can be our best teachers. We can ask ourselves, "How can I learn from this experience?" That's part of the process of those who cross the finish line. Going through the process is what matters. Once you understand that, whatever response you get will be OK; the negative ones will fade from your memory. You'll remember the "yesses" and what you learned from the "noes."

Your goals need to include not only how many times you'll show-the-plan but also how many people you'll sponsor. Just focus on your goals and each result will be of little consequence. *You, not the answer, control your destiny.* You'll find those who are to be in your group and you can keep growing as you go from one pin level to the next.

T

Chapter Ten

Talk Is Cheap

"When a person is down in the world, an ounce of help is better than a pound of preaching."
Edward Bulwer-Lytton

"Just Do As I Say" Doesn't Work

Some people who've experienced some success sponsoring people, after showing the plan a few times, let it "go-to-their-head." They may even believe that since they're now "experienced," they know it all. They think they're an absolute authority on every aspect of success! (Only recently they were quaking in their shoes as they made their first contact.) You need to be alert to any tendency like that you or someone in your group may have experienced. If so, it needs to be dealt with before it gets out of hand and has a negative affect on others in your group.

What sometimes happens is a distributor begins to act a lot like a teenager trying to break free from their parents. They insist that they're mature (in a business sense) enough to begin directing their group. They want the same independence that the distributors who have reached the top have. They want to "teach" their people all they have learned. They may think they don't need to counsel with their Direct – now that "they know what they're doing."

You're Not Their Boss

You need to be careful. Legally, all the distributors own their distributorship – they're in their own business. Of course, our corporate supplier has a code of ethics and some "do's" and "don'ts" we all need to follow to maintain our distributorships.

As a cooperative team, each leadership organization is likely to have schedules of activities – open meetings, training sessions, seminars, rallies, and other miscellaneous events which are optional for each distributor. People who are serious about building their business certainly can benefit from following upline recommendations regarding attendance at such events.

You need to remember that you aren't anyone's boss in this business and no one is your boss. So, in essence, you have no right to demand anything from your distributors. Most distributors already have a job or another business of their own where there are lots of demands. In some cases, distributors don't know how to handle the independence that this business gives them and may need your understanding to help them get things in perspective.

Since you're not their boss it isn't appropriate to simply tell them to listen and do as you say. You need to compliment what confidence in themselves you've observed and do your best to work within that confidence level to help them build the business. In the process you can help them develop and become more confident. The most effective way to teach them is by example. They can observe what you do to make this business work as well as what your upline leaders do. Whenever you can, as you're teaching your downline, edify the upline people who are helping you to be successful. This will appropriately give your upline the credibility they deserve. In turn, your distributors are more likely to listen to their teachings, and edify *you* to *their* group.

Point out, as often as possible, that you are where you are because you follow-the-system and listen to the counsel of upline. Also let them know how important duplication is. It makes it possible for a lot of different people with varied talents and skills to build the business. Explain that while they may be better equipped at building this business than you were, those who they sponsor may not be as talented. By following and teaching the system, they'll set a powerful example for everyone in their group to follow.

Saying "NEXT!" To One Who's Already "In"

Even when you do everything we've just talked about, some people may still want independence. Whenever you're associated with a large group of people, you're likely to find some who'll constantly go against the grain. In this case, they probably won't want to follow the system. Understand, the more people you sponsor, the more you're likely to run into these people. So you might as well be prepared.

While they may be a small minority, you may still have the tendency to want to *convert* them to the system. Afterall, you want to see them achieve their true potential. What you need to realize, however, is that you may see their potential before they do. And, of course, you know that by following-the-system, they'll dramatically increase their likelihood of success. Be patient. Your upline can give you ideas about what to do specifically with a particular distributor.

People who are independent by nature are generally intelligent. They're probably so used to doing things on their own, that they may not only fail to ask for help, but also resist help when it's offered. The more you do your best to help them, the more they may resist. Some of these people have pretty big egos that they've developed in the conventional business world. They don't yet have the humbleness it requires to be interdependent and work as a team. It's likely you'll need to give them some time to adjust to the idea of your working together.

Once they realize that a network is built by teamwork – that the power of duplication is one of its greatest benefits, they may be more likely to ask for help. They need to understand this business isn't like conventional businesses where they may have been completely on their own to "sink-or-swim." Before, they might have been in a win-lose situation. But now, in this business, they have a win-win scenario where there are "people-helping-people." You keep on moving – encouraging everyone, but waiting for no one.

Everyone who grows in the business does so at their own pace. Some could "take-off" and grow faster than you may now imagine. Others will take longer, perhaps, because they need to overcome more obstacles. The system teaches you how to be patient with people. For example, sponsor a lot of people so you're less inclined to let it bother you if someone won't listen. You'll have plenty of people who will.

Everyone comes in with a different level of understanding. Some know the principles of success and have used these ideas to achieve in other areas. Then, on the other end of the spectrum, some have little, if any, understanding of how to be successful. As people follow-the-system in the business, they can grow in whatever areas they need to grow.

You just keep on going – believing in everyone, but not letting anyone hold you back from accomplishing your goals and dreams. You find those who want to "go" who are serious. The ones who aren't may change their thinking as they experience more of life's challenges and continue developing through the teachings of the system. This is true for independent thinkers too. There's hope for everyone, as long as they persist, that they can make those cherished goals and dreams come true.

If one of your distributors tells you they're going to build the business alone and doesn't want to listen, you could ask upline what to do. You may be advised to back off some for now. Remember, "You can't push a rope. You can't nail Jell-O® to the wall. And you can't make a dead dog walk. But you *can* gently lead a wet noodle!" They may be just a "wet noodle" who has had some negative experiences in the conventional business world that caused them to be defensive in their attitude.

Some of the biggest rewards in this business were achieved by such people who grew to trust and follow-the-system after some rough times getting adjusted in the beginning. They may be a "Diamond in the rough"! Let those people know, as you do other distributors, that you're willing to help any member of their group who needs it. Keep in touch with those in their group who may be more immediately teachable! (In some cases, when your upline has been helping you build depth, you'll need to work it out with them as to who helps who.) Help others to win and you'll win too. Remember, being successful means growing through these challenges!

That independent person may appreciate the space you're giving them to do what they believe they need to do. As a result, they might be more receptive to suggestions in the future. Their change in attitude could occur when you help one of their people build the business. Say one of their distributors begins to grow more quickly because they're listening to you and following the system. Who knows – maybe the independent distributor will want better results and decide to plug into the system afterall! And because you treated them with respect and didn't push them, it may be easier for them to come to you for help.

If one of your distributors takes a new direction, away from the proven system, regardless of exactly what happens, you need to consider the rest of the group. The independent person is simply one who *got "in"* and then, possibly, said, "No," either directly or through their actions. You need to be ready to say *"NEXT!"* and move-on with the distributors who *are* teachable and want to grow. Perhaps the independent person will come along later. If they don't, it's their loss and your gain.

Remember "Show and Tell"?

To simply tell someone what they *must* do, as we discussed before, is inappropriate since nobody *has* to do anything – the business is strictly voluntary. You also may get some difficult-to-answer questions if you make demands. They may ask you what you did and, especially if you don't have a big business yet, how come you aren't more successful? Why "must" they do certain things if they haven't made *you* successful yet? They just don't understand that everyone grows at a different rate. They're too busy being defensive, disliking being bossed around, to see the power of the system. So don't "should" on them – instead "could" them. Apologize and rephrase, if they're still willing to listen. Tell them this is a voluntary business and there's a proven success system that they can follow, if they choose to. It's totally up to them what they do – they're their own boss in this business!

Rather than put yourself on the defensive, *demonstrate to educate*. Show them what you've learned – do a role-play, write what you're teaching on paper or a white board, share some support material or whatever is appropriate. Then explain it. That doesn't mean the new lesson needs to have a successful conclusion in order for it to benefit your group.

For example, in showing someone how to show-the-plan, you may make some mistakes, especially if you've just learned how yourself. The fact that you took action, using what you learned, is all you need to drive home a point. It opens the door for discussion and allows the members of your group to see that failure at one attempt does not dictate the final outcome – it's just part of the learning process.

Sometimes it's even better to fail when you're teaching. It takes the stigma out of failure and makes you far more relatable and approachable. Then, if the people in your group fail at their first attempt, they're less likely to feel like failures. They'll tend to more readily accept it as a part of the learning process.

When you simply explain something to them, rather than demonstrating, they will often regard their failure as a reflection of their inability. This can result in them giving up on a new technique. It can also serve to foster resistance to new ideas in the future. We can often learn a lot about what *not* to do from our failures. That can be *extremely* valuable.

Are You *"Talking-The-Talk"* Or *"Walking-The-Walk"?*

Sometimes you might find someone in your group who, for whatever reason, seems to be looking to quit as soon as they get "in." They may have lost confidence in their ability after they got their first "no." Perhaps they're considered experts on their everyday job and are finding it difficult to be out of their comfort zone – learning something new. They might have forgotten their dreams and goals. Or, they might be influenced by outside forces – like negative thinking people. They can't quite bring themselves to quit for no reason – so they look for one.

If you often explain what to do in the business without showing them by building the business yourself, you could be giving them a reason. They may think you're just trying to get rich off their efforts. If they only have your words to go on and see no action, they begin forming their own opinion. It's often based on what those closest to them are telling them – which may be discouraging them. On the other hand, when they see you're *doing it* and believe you'll do whatever it takes to help them, they may gain confidence again. Regardless, you're doing your best to be an example worth following and to be of service to them.

Perhaps there are people of theirs you can work with. As you may know, working in depth is one way to light a "fire" under a reluctant distributor or distributor line. When their group starts growing, without their input, they often get excited and their level of belief rises. That's why it's so important to build depth under a new distributor as soon as you can. You're increasing the odds of finding some folks who'll take the business and run with it. Nothing succeeds like success!

I

Chapter Eleven

Inspect What You Expect
"You get what you focus on."

Watch What You're Doing

Once when I was finishing my basement, my son, who was only four at the time, decided to help. I was about to hammer a large nail into a support stud at an awkward angle, when he took his position. Toy hammer in hand, he placed himself between me and the wall and was ready to swing at the same time I was. I looked down to make sure he was safe and drove my thumb into the stud. Ouch!

As I uncrossed my eyes and saw the oddest shade of purple on my finger, I noticed my son hammering away at his nail. He never took his eyes off his objective. I, on the other hand, focused on something else and truly suffered the consequences.

"Yes" Or "No" – It Doesn't Matter

There's only one time when it's OK to take your eyes off your goal or destination – when you get there! Every other time you do it'll slow you down, drive you off course, or even get you totally lost. When you're passionate and committed about where you want to be and what you want to become, your focus needs to be crystal clear to get what you want.

Other people's responses aren't important. As the title of this book says, *"If they say 'no' just say NEXT!"* While that takes care of the negative responses, you also want to keep moving after you get a positive response. As tempting as it may be to celebrate and savor a "yes," after hanging-in-there through all the "noes," it will also slow you down in your quest. Both the "noes" and the "yesses" are just a part of the natural process of success.

Treat all answers equally. Whether they say "no," "yes," or "maybe," you need to be planning your next move. Focusing on any of these answers can really delay your progress. If someone says, "no," and you dwell on it, there's a tendency to analyze and reanalyze what you could have done differently. What might you have said? Is there any way you could have done better? It's important to learn from your experiences. But once you've done that, *let-it-go*. Let me clue you in. Sure, almost anybody can do a better job with hindsight. As movie director Billy Wilder once said, "Hindsight is always twenty-twenty." But the fact is it's probably not anything *you* said or did that caused them to say "no." Often that person is letting other issues that you're probably unaware of hold them back.

One of the mistakes I made in the beginning was celebrating each "yes." I know it's recommended that we book a couple of meetings when we get agreement – but instead, I just wanted to savor the moment. I was also afraid that if I pushed too hard I might turn the "yes" into a "no." What happened was many of these "yesses" became one person "groups," who soon faded away.

Here's a few reasons for setting-up a couple of meetings when the prospective distributor says "yes." First, this helps get them started in the system. Second, this shows them you're doing whatever-it-takes to help them. Third, it's to build a group under them which proves the system works. Fourth, perhaps they aren't really serious about building the business, but someone under them may be hungry to move-on. Finally, and often overlooked, it takes you away from reveling in the glory of a recent "yes" and keeps you on-track toward your destination!

How Will You Know When You Get There?

There's an old cliché – *"If you don't know where you're going, you'll probably end up someplace else."* Most people aren't aiming for anything except just getting through each day – that's called survival. So guess what they get? Survival, usually, and maybe not even that. I'm sure you agree that's no way to live.

So, to "rise-above-the-crowd," you need to keep your destination in the forefront. Do what you know you need to do to bring yourself closer and closer to reaching your goals. Keep persisting through the challenges, doing whatever-it-takes. When you reach a goal or dream, go ahead and celebrate. You deserve it. You've done what few people do. You set your sights and completed your mission – or at least part of it. You blasted through obstacles. You weathered the delays with the faith that each would pass. You adjusted your attitude if you became discouraged. You kept focused on what you wanted to do and you did it! So now it's time to keep going, building on your success until you accomplish your next goal or dream. Dream bigger after each victory! That's what winners do!

There are people who are successful, in everyone else's opinion but their own. And it's only their opinion that counts in this matter! Since they were never clear with themselves as to where they wanted to end up, they were never sure if they got there. Sure, they accomplished some notable things. But was what they achieved what they *really, really, really* wanted? Or was it what *someone else* wanted? Like the boss? How much greater could it have been for them had they focused their energy in the direction of *their* dreams?

I'd rather come close to a goal that *I* had set, then spend my life never knowing the feeling of arriving at or even getting near a destination of my choice. How about you? If people are always doing what somebody else wants, they're likely to be constantly asking, "Is this all there is?" They don't know the joy of clearly defining a goal, doing whatever-it-takes to make it happen, and enjoying the fruits of their efforts.

What If...?

What if there was an exact formula for arriving at your destination? Would you follow it? More than likely you would because you're in this business to reach some goals. There probably wouldn't be too many questions on your part either. Once you figure out exactly what you need to do to reach your goal, what else would you need to know?

For example, if your goal requires that you talk to 1,000 people, would you do it? I know that seems like a lot, but let's say you're seeking total financial freedom and that's the number of people you need to see to do it. Break it down. If you saw just two people a day, you'd be financially free in less than a year and a half. Now could you do it?

That's just an example (rather than a real formula), but notice one very important aspect of what you just read. *There was absolutely no reference to how many people needed to say "yes" for you to achieve your goal!* Dwelling on the "noes" only slows you down. You need to just keep on going. In this example, when you talk to 1,000 people, there would probably be plenty who say, "yes" and chances are, you'd reach your goal. Exactly how many "yesses" would you get? Does it really matter?

It's like playing tennis. How many balls does a player have to hit across the net to win the game? Nobody ever counts, do they? And your success in this business is the same way. "Just keep hitting the ball over the net."

> *"Anything worth having is worth striving for with all your might."*
> Orville Redenbacher

N

Chapter Twelve

Need To Succeed

"The successful person is the one who forms the habit of doing what the failing person doesn't do."
Donald Riggs

Do What You "Gotta" Do

Take out a piece of paper. Write down exactly why you got "in" this business in the first place. Do your best to remember what went through your mind the moment you decided you were going to do this. There's no right or wrong answer. You may not even be able to recall what you were thinking. That's OK, too.

Where has your focus been lately? Has it changed? If it has, it may be because you have bigger dreams now. For others, it may be that you've simply forgotten why you're doing this, and that fact may be slowing your growth.

Regardless of where your focus has taken you, to be truly successful, you need to be committed to achieving your goals and dreams. Focusing on what you want helps you to keep going, overcoming any obstacles you encounter along the way.

When I was writing my first book, I constantly focused on my dream of seeing it in the hands of many people. That helped me to stay motivated, especially on the days where the words weren't coming. It helped me focus on the quality of each chapter. It also helped me deal with the rejections I received from publishers around the country. I kept my dream alive by focusing on it.

Once I finished writing, I began sending out proposals to different publishers. With each one I mailed, I envisioned their logo on my book in the hands of many readers. Then I would picture the book without any logo on it, but still being read by millions. I was determined to succeed. Nothing was going to stop me.

The beauty of my quest was that I only needed one publisher to say "yes" to my idea and I was on my way. With that in mind, each rejection only meant that particular publisher wasn't going to share in my success. That attitude kept me going. It wasn't until after 99 rejection letters that I found a believer! And that's why this book is in your hands.

The other important aspect of your need to succeed is the "amnesia" that occurs once you arrive. As I saw the first copies of my book in the hands of readers literally around the world, the "amnesia" hit. To this day, I can't remember the name of one single editor who turned down my idea. The "noes" just don't matter. That's what happens to you when you simply keep heading for your dream destination rather than from answer to answer.

Spread The Word

When you need some help sticking to something when it seems as if nothing is going right, tell the upline person who's helping you that you're going to make it. Not only will that act as a positive affirmation for you, it will also help you persist, even when it's difficult. Many people are just as motivated to avoid pain, fear, and embarrassment as they are to gain recognition and success. They'd rather keep going through the "noes" until they get to the "yesses." It's easier than having to admit to the person they told they were going to make it, that they failed or gave up. How about you?

Telling someone upline how serious you are about your financial future also has another advantage. You can ask for their support when you need it. They can encourage you to "pick-yourself-up, dust-yourself-off, and-start-all-over-again." They can help you focus on your dreams and goals. They can recommend books for you to read to develop in certain areas and tapes that will help you stay motivated. They'll suggest you attend certain functions where you can learn from leaders and mix with other people who are moving-on and excited about life. This can help you stay fired-up and grow in the direction of your goals and dreams. If you're feeling "down," go upline (you don't want to pass negative downline). And when you're "up," you can share the excitement with upline, as well as downline!

Support + Individual Success = System Strength

Once you've made a decision to begin your trip toward you dreams and goals, you're already being successful. The journey *is* the success! You've separated yourself from the average-thinking crowd and you've begun your trip to the top. Along the way, it's likely you'll encounter some challenges. Every successful person is presented with their biggest opportunities to grow, when they meet their difficulties head-on and overcome them. And along the line, you'll also have many small and some big victories as well.

As part of a large support team, you will be recognized at each step along the way. These pats on the back can help sustain you as you reach for the next level. Drive for each of them and then use each one to build your confidence to propel you towards the next step. You will discover that these are not so much individual milestones but a continuous, cumulative testimony to your drive coupled with the power of the system. Each achievement adds to the previous ones, bringing you ever closer to your final goal.

The system thrives and grows stronger as more and more people become successful. It has a vested interest in your success. In fact, most of its efforts are directed at your succeeding because when that happens, the success of the whole system is enhanced.

"If it is to be, it's up to me."
Tom Smith

G

Chapter Thirteen

Greatness Comes From Giving

"Maturity begins to grow when you can sense your concern for others outweighing your concern for yourself."
John MacNaughton

Sponsor Yourself Every Day

If you were to meet yourself right now, would you want *you* in your business? This isn't a silly question. In fact, it's essential that you often ask yourself that question. When you do, you'll find yourself evaluating your attitude from a different, but very important perspective. By looking at yourself from the outside in, you'll be better able to see what those in your group, as well as the new people you're meeting, see.

If you wouldn't want yourself in your group, why would those around you want to be in business with you? This becomes one of those "perception is reality" deals. Whatever those around you perceive about you becomes who you are in their minds. When you're building any type of organization, what is thought about you affects the success of the organization. Are you a motivated example who's following the system?

Fortunately, this is one area that's fairly simple to correct, if necessary. Sponsor yourself every day. Remember the enthusiasm you had when you first got "in"? You were excited, weren't you? When you're showing-the-plan (whether it's to one person or a group of people), talk as if what you say will determine if *you* want to get "in." When you've finished a meeting with this intention, you'll have a 100% success rate. You'll sponsor someone at every plan you ever show, even if it's just yourself!

What If They Ask How I'm Doing?

You may be just getting started. Say you've chosen this business as your vehicle to financial and time freedom. Following the system, you begin sharing the idea with others. Then at your first real meeting, a negative-thinking person asks this: "Before I get involved, how are *you* doing?" Many new distributors, who may even have some notable success in other arenas, don't know quite how to respond.

If you tell them, "I'm just getting started," even though it's true, it sounds weak and won't be of much help to them. Instead you need to communicate your confidence in the business. Just because you may not have a track record yet, doesn't affect the potential for your prospects. They'll have the same access to the system that you do, which has helped a lot of people achieve their goals and dreams. It can help your prospect too, even if they're overly cautious in the beginning. Your attitude is important; their response isn't. Remember, *"If they say 'no,' just say 'NEXT!'"* If they say, "no," it's their loss. Someone else will say, "yes," and it'll be their gain. You've got a dream to reach for and you aren't going to let anything or anybody get in the way.

What you don't want is for your prospect to use your response as an excuse to delay getting "in" the business. By saying you're just starting, you could invite an answer of, "Call me when you're successful." They don't understand that you've already achieved a degree of success simply by deciding to change your life; that was your first step. You became even more successful when you made the commitment to build the business and started taking action to reach your goals and dreams.

Here's an answer that you can use that may help your prospect. It's honest, supports them in reaching *their* potential, and takes the focus off you and puts it on them.

Prospect: "So how are you doing at this thing?"

You: "Telling you how I'm doing may give the impression that this is as good as it gets. One of the benefits of this business is that you can achieve as much as you want. You may not need to change your life as much as I do, while others may need more change and will not be held back by what I achieve. You can build a bigger business than me, just like other people I've sponsored can. You tell me what level of success *you* want to achieve, and I can show you people you can relate to who have done it."

That answer isn't only powerful but it's most certainly the truth. You're also sharing the principles of Free Enterprise with them. Unlike most people with a job, they can create whatever income they need to accomplish their goals and dreams.

Is It Better To Give Than Receive?

I think both giving and receiving are pretty good events. To say which one is better often depends on your perspective. If you are in a place in life where you have been doing without due to financial struggles, receiving something may be just the thing to change your life. So, receiving is good.

If you have been blessed with an abundance of wealth or talent and you freely share with as many people as possible, there is a tremendous feeling of satisfaction in giving. In this case, giving is good.

The state our minds are in will determine which one is better. Your state of mind when either one is happening will either speed or slow your business development. For example, if you only sponsor people into the business solely for the purpose of getting you where you want to go, it'll take a long time, if ever, before you see any growth.

Yet, when you learn to give, focusing on helping others, while expecting absolutely nothing in return, you could experience tremendous growth both financially as well as personally. Sometimes you only need to make a small difference in a few people's lives to have a huge impact on your own. Maybe that difference is that you showed them you care about them and their success.

Let's use some real numbers both ways. First, we'll assume that you have a burning desire to get to 7,500. Say you want to become a Direct Distributor and you're so focused that nothing will stop you. You begin to prospect for people with only *your* dreams in mind. If your attitude is to get them "in" the business to reach *your* dreams, you may scare some people away! They can sense self-centeredness!

Those who get "in" are all at different levels of personal development and financial success and have different dreams than you. But you may not think that matters. You're focused on your dreams and on building a Direct distributorship, no matter what. The tendency is to push your people into having more meetings, prospecting daily, and calling to see what they've done for you today. Some people may respond to that and could grow. However, with that kind of controlling behavior, most will begin to see this great opportunity as nothing more than another job. While they may need the additional income, most people don't want another boss!

On the other hand, when you listen to the dreams of those you sponsor and work to help them fulfill them, wonderful things can happen. I'll be overly simple here just to prove a point. Imagine the next ten people you sponsored all had the same dream. They each needed to earn about $200 a month to send their children to a better school. You felt that was a worthwhile goal and became determined to help each one achieve it.

Say that $200 in income is generated by doing 1,000 volume points. Let's say that during the next several months you make this happen for only ten people. You do this by giving unconditionally and focusing on your people rather than yourself. You'd be at 10,000 points per month with a group of ten very loyal distributors. When only three of them adopt your giving philosophy and each helps ten people achieve *their* dreams, your giving ways can result in your total financial freedom!

"The secret of living is giving."
Birdie Yager

C

Chapter Fourteen

Consider The Alternatives
"The choices you make on a daily basis affect what you will be, do, or have in the tomorrows of your life."

You May Be Doing "Pretty Good"

Things are probably going along fairly well. It's likely you pay all your bills, you provide for your family and you're not wanting for the necessities of life. You're taking care of your immediate financial responsibilities. That's terrific; we need more people to do that. But let me ask you this, "What if something happens to you tomorrow and you're unable to continue doing what you're doing? How long could you and your family survive?

Many people work hard to achieve a level of success that gives them a greater reward for their efforts. For those of us who are parents, we want the best for our kids and we're working to give them a comfortable home and to meet their needs. But as long as the signature on the front of your paycheck isn't yours, you're trading your time for dollars in order to get it. If you're like a lot of people, a large portion of that check probably goes to debt and you've delegated most of your control over your financial destiny to your boss. If, for some reason, you're no longer able to take care of your responsibilities, of course your family suffers.

It's true that what we've just covered are unpleasant realities. It's likely you wouldn't be in the business if you hadn't already given these ideas serious thought. Others may be willing to put up with having little control over their finances. Often they've sold their soul to the "company store." They may have convinced themselves that everything's "OK," but you know better.

You know they can create security for themselves and their family through this business as well as make their dreams come true. You know what you have your hands on with this business. Just because some of the people you talk to accept mediocrity, doesn't mean you have to let them influence you. You stick to your convictions. Maybe eventually they'll figure it out as they see you building your business and moving-on – that they can do it too. Then *they* can come to *you* for help!

Who's In Control, You or "No"?

When you begin succeeding in this business (which happens the moment you say "yes" and start taking action in the direction of your dreams), your feeling of control over your destiny begins to grow. As long as you maintain that control, life can be a joy. It doesn't matter how big your business is now or how big it becomes. That control is the essence of what you will attain. Protect it at all cost.

When you have get-togethers (meetings) to share this business, remember who has control. If twenty people show up and they all decide this isn't for them, maintain control. Letting their answers affect your next move, allows "the committee of they" to retake control of your life.

I can't stress enough that you aren't looking for any one particular person. You're searching for enough people who need and want your help. (You'll know what "enough" is as you reach your goals and dreams.) When you truly believe you can help people with this opportunity, you won't let a few "noes" get in the way of finding and helping them.

Success Takes Time

How long have you been doing what you're doing? I sat down and wrote my first book in 1987. To date I'm the only one who's seen it. I read it the other day and realized my son can write better and he's only 12. Three years later I had my first article published. A year after that I contributed a chapter to someone else's book. Then in 1997, I finally had my first book published – 10 years after my first attempt! It took 10 years to get where I wanted to go. There are two points in telling you my story – I knew I'd get there and the time it took was irrelevant. Know that *you* can make it too, as long as you keep persisting. And realize that it'll take whatever time it takes to get the job done.

There's flexibility in that this business allows you to arrive at your own pace. (The fact remains though, that when you pick up your pace, you can develop momentum more quickly.) You may grow faster than some and perhaps slower than others. But as long as you keep going – consistently doing business-building activities, staying plugged-into-the-system, and fine-tuning your skills along the way, you will arrive. Most people forget that it also took them some time to acquire the knowledge and skills that got them to where they are at work or in their own (other) business. Gaining success in this business is similar. And even though it's simple, it does take effort. To build anything securely, it takes time and energy. Be patient. Nothing great happens overnight. As Dr. Robert Schuller says in his book *If It's Going To Be It's Up To Me,* "Every achievement is a process, not an instamatic happening."

One of the advantages of this opportunity is that you can build your business as you learn. You're qualified to use any tool or technique as soon as it's presented to you. With the support system that's in place, it helps to carry you so your business can grow even when you make mistakes!

To be a successful entrepreneur, you need to eliminate any Monday-thru-Friday paycheck mentality that you may have. You need to invest a certain amount of your time and energy into your business before you get the rewards. Look at all the super-successful examples that you can follow. How did they make this transition? Ask them the questions that will help you grow. They're happy to help. Yet, there's one question that is never heard asked of these leaders – "How long did it take you to get there?" Other than to give people hope, it really doesn't matter. What's important is that they hung in there through the challenges to make it happen; one-day-at-a-time.

It's an "infinite-way-tie" for first place. Everyone who strives for their destination and doesn't quit, wins. There's no time limit on success. Upon your arrival, you'll be greeted with the same respect and celebration, whether it took you two years or twenty. Everyone's just glad you made it.

Of Course, There's No Obligation

No one can make you do this. In fact, no one can make you do anything. What you choose to do is entirely up to you. You can choose to grow or not to grow. You can choose to build the business or to simply work your job and maintain your life like it is. The thing of it is though, choosing the status quo will also allow you to predict the future.

Take a look at what you currently do for a living. Unless you're the first and only one to do it, there's a certain path your career is likely to follow. To predict where you'll be in five, ten, or fifteen years, just look at someone of similar qualifications, who's already been doing it that long. That'll give you a pretty good idea where you'll be after a period of time.

Say you could allow yourself to be discouraged by a couple of negative responses from people who aren't ready to build the business yet. You decide to get a part-time job rather than face further rejection. The first thing you'd lose is the time savings you were beginning to accumulate due to leveraging with your distributors. The second thing you'd give up is the association with positive-thinking people who, like you, want to win. Most importantly, you'd give up the possibilities that the business holds for you and your family.

By going forward, knowing the potential this business has for you, even though a few people said "no," means you're taking control of your life. *You* (not the negative responses and the fear of future rejection) are now in control. Just like the feelings of accomplishment that grow with each "yes," these negative feelings will diminish with each rejection. You're focusing on your goal – not the potential rejection. You refuse to avoid rejection. You know that every achiever faces rejection along the way. *You've got the faith and courage that you, too, will make it because you're not giving up.*

Like all of us, you receive the results of your choices each day. The beauty is that when you decide to succeed at this business, make a firm commitment to do so, and consistently do what you need to do to make it work for you, you'll win. Since no one's forcing you or looking over your shoulder, you're doing it because *you* want to. Choosing to do something *on your schedule* with the people *you want to associate with* certainly makes it easier to stay motivated, regardless of a few negative responses along the way.

"Character is the ability to carry out a good resolution long after the excitement of the moment has passed."
Cavett Robert

L

Chapter Fifteen

Let Them Lead Where You Want To Go

"The most infectiously joyous men and women are those who forget themselves in thinking about and serving others."
Robert J. McCracken

Who Wants Another Job?

Say you've sponsored a few people who seem to be interested in changing their lives. What do you do? You could tell them to set up some meetings. Tell them how to prospect. Let them know what's expected of them. Compare them to others. Tell them where they have to be and when. Sound familiar? What's wrong with this picture?

For those of you who work for someone else, it probably sounds a lot like your job. For those of you in conventional business, it's likely it sounds similar to how you lead your employees. You need to understand, above all else, a distributor is *not* an employee of yours. They didn't get "in" to be dictated to. In most cases, they already put up with that on their jobs. Some are satisfied with their jobs, but need more money. And some people simply hate their work. They certainly don't want more pressure from their upline in this business than they're already getting at work.

Many are looking at this as the best hope they have of *escaping* from their jobs. If they're bossed around like they are at work, they may figure this business is like having a second job – which was *not* what they were looking for when they got "in." Besides, this would be like starting over. At least at work they're probably already *somewhere* up the ladder – with their seniority perhaps, if nothing else.

Show Them The "Map"

When you invest the time to find out exactly what it is they want and how quickly they want to get there, it'll be much simpler to help them get on-track. You can show them the basics. If you're not a Direct, check upline to determine who would counsel them on the specifics of what they need to do to get where *they* want to go. They can prove they're serious about building the business by their commitment to following the system and doing whatever it takes to get there.

The most important ingredient in successfully supporting your people, is to let them know that you'll be there for them. When they don't feel confident about trying something new, they need to know they can watch you do it for them first, then they can do it while you watch so they can get the hang of it. If they can't seem to get their own group going in the right direction, they need to be able to count on you to help them get it going. (In this process, you may need help from your upline – depending on how experienced you are in building the business.)

If they don't seem to want your help, it's OK to explain to them that you understand and have others that do want your help. Do it in such a kind, positive way, that if things change, they're likely to contact you. Always leave the door open to them. It could pay off for both of you down the road.

If you sense they're not serious about building the business, find out if they have some prospects that you could sponsor for them. Keep going through the "noes," both to sponsor frontline people and people in depth. Move-on and help those who are serious.

In the meantime, if they still won't budge, tell them you understand. Remember, there may be some other people who need your help, and now you're freed up to attend to them. (This will always be true – there will *always* be folks who need your help whether they're "in" or not!) Don't "burn-your-bridges" to those who may later decide to become active and build the business. Be pleasant, considerate, and easily approachable.

Hang On For A Great Ride

Give your people your vote of confidence. It could go a long way toward helping them to get the courage to begin growing. Be sincere in your desire to see them go to the level they want to achieve. Encourage them. Help them to get through any initial nervousness. It's likely they'll be less afraid of doing something new because they know you'll be there to help them do the right thing.

Focusing on helping your distributors reach their goals will help you to stay positive. If one of your groups slows down, it won't bother you as much because you can go work with another. You will find that as you get one of the other groups growing, an idea could come to you that may help you fire up the other group. Or maybe a little friendly competition will spur them on.

As you teach the leaders in your group the principle of helping others achieve their goals, you can leverage your effectiveness. You can progress more quickly with the same effort, as you get duplication. This is the *secret of the system*. By focusing on enough other people and helping them achieve their goals and dreams, you'll achieve *your* goals and dreams.

The success principles you instill and strengthen in others by staying plugged-into-the-system and plugging others in will compound itself in your own fulfillment. By turning your attention from yourself to helping those in your group succeed, you can ignore any distractions along the line. This makes it easier to concentrate on the outcomes you're working toward in each group. You're maintaining a positive attitude by counseling with your upline and staying plugged into the system, and taking consistent action toward your goals and dreams.

Really Mean It

When you share with a new person that they can achieve *their* dreams with this business – be sincere. As you're helping them get started, focus on doing what's best for *them* in terms of what *they* want to accomplish, rather than focusing on your goals. Help them understand that it's *their* business and that as long as they keep on persisting, they can reach whatever level they want. If you're ever tempted to treat them like an employee and boss them around, stop yourself. You don't want *them* to say "NEXT!" to *you* and to start looking for another opportunity, do you?

To achieve fast growth, you need to do whatever it takes to help your people reach their goals and dreams. Along the way they'll increase their self-confidence and faith in the business as they grow into leaders. This, in turn, will have a positive, motivating, impact on their group, keeping them fired up. Your integrity as a leader will be obvious and you'll generate respect. Others may refer people to you because of your successful track record. As your group grows and you rise through the pin levels, your momentum can increase.

How could your momentum increase? This occurs when people who put their faith in you achieve what they set out to do and then go for even bigger dreams. Because you unselfishly helped them accomplish their goals, they feel comfortable asking you to help them again. Only now they just need to sit down with you and discuss what to do next. (Depending on your pin level, you may need to refer them to an upline Direct for counseling.) They can then go and carry out their plan of action.

Such distributors are loyal followers of the system and upline leadership. They trust that you have their best interests at heart and continue to build momentum as duplication in their group grows. They're following your example, developing strong leaders of their own. As they grow, you grow!

As a final note to this chapter, I'm going to quote Dr. David Schwartz from his book *The Magic of Thinking Success:*

> *"Learn this principle of achievement well: We are successful in direct proportion to how well we motivate other people. What we gain in*

money, influence, and power depends on what we cause other people to do.... In whatever we do, we must have the support of others. To advance yourself through other people requires winning their cooperation. And the help of others must be voluntary. You can't force people to support you. Nor will you gain much by begging or pleading."

O

Chapter Sixteen

Only the Strong Can Serve

The Example You Set Will Speak For You

Success is attractive to people. They like to hang around a winner. They often want to learn the "secrets" of your success. How can you expect people to hang around if none of them know about your accomplishments?

It may appear that there's a dilemma. Yet the louder you shout about your accomplishments, the less admirable you'll appear to be. You'll also appear to be arrogant (which is not an endearing quality, by the way). Also, you certainly wouldn't be showing that you're humble – a characteristic that is key to your success. We all need to keep our ego in line and be appreciative of all the help we received along the way. *No one* succeeds alone. So how can others celebrate in your success, if you don't tell them about it? Let others do your talking for you!

Set a good example and spend time helping others succeed. When you serve their needs and offer assistance to your leaders, they will talk about you and your service. What begins as a slight murmur, can become a thunderous announcement of your arrival. Keep on giving and "your day" will come.

Who Are You Hanging Out With?

Would you like to spend more time with the leaders in your organization? The knowledge you would gain could surely help you go to the top. Yet, what could be holding you back?

Have you ever felt that while they may not have as much time to spend with you as you'd like, it would be nice to get more attention? When it starts to bother you, take a good look at what's going on. Notice how those who seem to get upline's time are those whose groups are growing the fastest. Are they part of an elite group of favorites or what? Not really.

They are building the dreams of others in their group who are not only asking for help but are also doing the business. *The basic idea here is that upline will match your efforts. When they see you really want the business by what you are doing, they will gladly help.* Then you'll get to spend more time with them!

Open opportunity meetings are examples of how the leaders serve you and your group. The leaders also provide major functions, seminars, training sessions, and other miscellaneous events to help you grow and achieve your dreams. The leaders in this business are service-oriented and dedicated. They're extraordinary and what they give is rare and unsurpassed anywhere else in the world.

When you associate with people who are serving others and helping them reach their potential so they can become successful, you'll begin to better understand the power of service. The success that you can achieve from helping others is incredible. You not only receive time and money rewards, but the deep sense of satisfaction that you're making a positive difference. There's no price you can put on the happiness you feel when you reach out and truly help someone have a better life. And, of course, giving is receiving. Your financial future is affected by how many people you bring into the business *and* help to be successful – plain and simple.

It's Easy To Feel "Up"

Helping others achieve even small successes will do wonders for your attitude. As you grow in the business, you'll find that you're more consistently positive – even on your most challenging days! Your great attitude and commitment to helping others succeed will attract success to you. Success is contagious and, like a magnet, it attracts more success to it! When you're focusing your efforts on helping others become successful, it's easier to have a great day, every day!

When your efforts are helping to create even little successes throughout your organization, your hope for your future increases. Even if some of your people slow down or give-up, you'll have enough other people moving-on and counting on you. As they share their little and big accomplishments with you, you'll be better able to weather any storm by keeping a positive solution-oriented attitude. It really helps to know you're making a difference and moving-on.

There's strength in numbers. By increasing the successes in your group, you'll fire others up to do the same. Just like when you learned to leverage your time "to be in more than one place at a time," you will be succeeding in places you've never even been to! Won't that be exciting?

What's The One Thing That Could Be Stopping You?

If you want the feeling of accomplishment that comes with success, you need to first learn to serve many people. *You need to become a student of the business so you can learn what to teach and duplicate.* You need to increase your business-building skills by doing what the system teaches until you master it. Then you can become an excellent example for others. It's that simple.

Just like anything else you've achieved in the past, you listened to the experts and kept at it until you learned it. Then you could, in turn, become the "expert" yourself and teach others. Other people of all ages and backgrounds who are no smarter than you have built this business. And you can too! Just follow-the-system as if your life depends on it and you'll experience your life changing for the better. Mine has and yours can too!

What could possibly be holding you back? Are you remembering your mission? You need to keep your dream in sight, be solidly committed to it, and know basically what it'll take to get you there. As you focus on your dream, you need to be steadily and enthusiastically following "the-pattern-of-success" – the system. Observe those who are succeeding in the business. They're focused like a laser beam, aren't they? They're fired up in a big way about achieving their dreams. How are they doing it? They're taking their eyes off themselves and are helping others build the business. They're people who care about others and they're dedicated followers of the system. How about you?

First, picture yourself as a determined winner. Now, suppose someone you respect and were counting on to get-in said they weren't interested? They even went so far as to say this "thing" couldn't work and is only for "suckers." As a student of success, would you dwell on their "no"? Absolutely not! You'd say, "NEXT!" You'd certainly wish them well and leave the door open for them to change their mind. But you wouldn't let such a negative-thinking person affect *your* long-term success. No way! You *know* what you've got your hands on.

You did your best to communicate the potential of this business to them. That's all you can do – except prove it by building a big business yourself! You know that someday they can "eat-their-words," while you laugh all the way to the bank! They say you either build the business because you're angry about the way things are; you're excited about the way things could be; or both. And I bet you're both! You'll show them!

You call upline and share your experience. You're reassured that everyone who becomes successful gets lots of "noes." You find out you're not alone. You also learn what, if anything, you could have done better. You listen to any tapes and read any books upline recommends to help you. You bounce back with more determination than ever!

If you get a hard "no" (one that's particularly difficult to accept), in addition to talking to upline, there are some other things you can do. Do some heavy dreambuilding – drive your favorite car, tour your dream house, watch a video of your dream trip, or something else. Keep contacting people and showing-the-plan to find the "yesses." Go help some of the other people in your group grow. Read more recommended books and listen to more tapes to keep yourself on the right track – give yourself a double dose of motivation! You'll be amazed at how quickly you can overcome your disappointments and move-on. You're becoming more and more resilient!

Focus on the positive and let go of the negative. The longer you dwell on any negative situation in life, the more energy you're giving it and the bigger it seems to get in your mind. If someone turns this opportunity down, remember, in most cases, they're saying "no" to the idea, for whatever reason, not because they're rejecting you. Let-it-go, wish them the best, and the whole incident will fade in your memory. Afterall, what kind of importance to your business does a person have who isn't interested in becoming a distributor, or at least a customer? What's the point in focusing on them?

You just need to know that the business works as long as you persistently work it. The rewards are given to those who have enough faith in themselves and the business so that they *stay on-track and keep-following-the-system,* regardless of what their prospects decide to do. Do you want your dreams hinging on what your prospects say? That would be delegating control of your future to people who probably don't have your best interests at heart.

Remember, shout it if you need to, but just say "NEXT!" Focus on your dreams and goals as your reasons and keep on going. You can do it! As Norman Vincent Peale's book is titled, *You Can If You Think You Can.*

S

Chapter Seventeen

Start Spreading The News

"An unshared life is not living. He who shares does not lessen, but greatens, his life."
Stephen S. Wise

If They Only Knew What You Know

The major purpose of this book is to help you to move beyond anyone who gives you a negative response and to go share the business with someone else. Yet, if you think for a minute about some of the "noes" you've gotten, you may notice there's a common theme. Some of those people may have said they weren't interested because, "I heard bad things...." or "I heard it's...." or even, "Isn't this illegal? I heard it was."

Many of you may have heard the same stories yet you still got "in." How come? More than likely, some people you respected talked to you and gave you a true picture of what this business is all about. You probably heard that this is an organization based on sound business principles, integrity, and people helping people.

Where do these stories come from? In a lot of cases they sprout from people's unwillingness to take responsibility for their own success. They may be active for a short time in the business. Then they get some "noes," as anyone in this or any other business will. It's just part of the weeding-out process. They may not understand that persistence is key to success in anything. Instead of blasting through the "noes," they look for someone or something else to blame. Then they crawl right back into their comfort zone of inactivity. They're likely to talk to others, planting seeds of doubt and fear in the minds of those who lack the knowledge and confidence to realize what's happening. These "dream stealers" put down the very opportunity that, had they hung in there and kept going, could very well have been the key to their financial future.

There are naysayers everywhere. They're often people who don't have the courage to follow their own dreams. They're like crabs in a pail – when one begins to crawl up the side to get out, the others pull him back in. It's a "misery loves company" mentality that causes them to try to steal other people's dreams. This is one of the reasons why it's so important to *stay positive and plugged-into-the-system*. It helps you to stay strong and determined for yourself and others in the face of negative-thinking people. We all need encouragement – someone to believe in us and tell us, "You can do it!" The system provides such support. Just keep on going, following the system, and hanging around others who are moving-on too. Your skills will develop and your self-confidence will grow.

Plant Different Seeds And Use "Super Grow"

Suppose you don't like what you're hearing from these negative-thinking people? In fact, you're beginning to get tired of it. Is there anything you can do? *If you don't like what's growing in your garden, plant different seeds.*

Do this experiment. For the next thirty days spend five minutes thinking one single thought. Before you go to bed each night, clear your mind for just five minutes and focus on only one idea. The "idea" is a serious illness that will happen to you. Do this for thirty days.

When I tell that to groups I'm speaking to they all look at me like I'm crazy. They protest telling me that it's truly possible to cause sickness when you concentrate on it long enough. They're correct. DO NOT DO THIS! It was just to get your attention and open your mind to what's coming.

Why do most people always seem to believe that the worst thing can happen to them, but never the best? Have you been conditioned to think that good things occur only to *other* people? Has the seed of fear grown and spread to choke out your entire garden? The great news is that by just associating with the people in this business, you've begun planting a new crop. Now you need to weed it and feed it.

By now, you have an idea of how far you'd like to go in this business (the seed). Picture yourself there. What changes will take place in your life? What type of people will you be hanging around with (fertilizer)? What type of person will you become (weed killer)?

Now for some "Super Grow." When you think about who you will be and who you will know, what changes can you make right now toward achieving that? What can you do today that is more like the person you're becoming than the person you've been in the past? Once you can answer that, do it!

You may find it difficult to determine which is occurring first – are you becoming successful and changing or are you changing and becoming successful? I'm not sure it matters, as long as the change occurs. More than likely though, it will be a combination of both.

All Eyes Are On You

When you make these mental changes, you will begin to get different reactions when you share this business with others. They may still say "no" but some of them will be less sure as to why they said it. People who've known you for a while will notice a change in you. Regardless of whether your prospects knew you before, they'll all respond to the change in you. And that will create changes in them.

Some of them, who may think they're looking out for you, will try to plant negative seeds in you in an effort to create fear of the "thing" you've joined, or the "brainwashing" that's occurred. (If they only knew it, their brains could use a good washing with positive-thinking motivational ideas!) Others will try to plant seeds of resentment because to them, you're one of the "other" people that good things happen to.

Still others will develop a strong jealousy. They'll want what you have but be afraid of leaving their "comfort zone," which could be more appropriately called their uncomfortable "familiar zone." Their friends may be going "nowhere fast" but they're still hanging-on to the "failure train" rather than getting on the "success train" with you. These folks are likely to watch you to see what you do and if your excitement lasts. This is where you'll experience growth when you just hang-in-there and keep on going.

Since many of them are likely to be watching you (even if they'd never admit it), why not give them a good show? If one says "no," move-on to the *"NEXT!"* person. When someone says "yes," plug them into the system, do what you can to help them, and move-on to the *"NEXT!"* person. As you achieve more success and are able to do more fun things with your time, some of those former naysayers might just humble themselves and come to see you!

GNN – The Good News Network

Based on what you've read so far, do you now understand how you can turn the negative around and be more fired up than ever? When you focus on your dream and helping others, rather than focusing on the effect an individual answer has on you, you can create positive change in your life and help others at the same time. (And one of the *best ways you can help your people* is to teach them how to get through the "noes" and get to the "yesses.")

As you continue down the road to where you want to go, you'll encounter many things. You'll be overcoming obstacles that would have stopped the less-determined. Always keep your goals and dreams in sight. You may stumble occasionally and have doubts about where you're heading. That's normal. You need to believe more in yourself and the system. To do this, read more books that are recommended by upline for personal and business development. Listen to more tapes available through the system – not just once but over-and-over. "Drill" these ideas into your mind. Repetition is the key to learning. Read the success stories of those who've already done it.

Know deep in your heart that you can build the business too. You can make your dreams come true. You just may need some counseling from your upline leader. Then you can dust yourself off, reset your sights on your objective, and you're on your way again. Some prospects may say "no" for themselves but give you some referrals. Graciously accept their help and encouragement and wish them well.

As your journey continues, some will want to join you along the way. As you bring each person into your group and you have more duplication-of-the-system, you'll gain momentum. Your success makes you more attractive to others. And, as some of them join you and build the business, your momentum will increase even more.

If you encounter obstacles, you know they're just part of the "game" of life and you take them in stride. You simply handle them as quickly as possible and keep on moving towards your goals. You know *nothing* is going to get in your way. You're keeping a positive attitude.

Some of the people who were totally against getting "in" are no longer sure they made the right decision. As your group and confidence grows, those observing you who used to doubt the validity of this business are likely to be less confident about what they said before. Instead of being stubbornly insistent about how these "things" never work, they may begin to change their minds. They might even approach you to see the plan again!

Some of them may even "give-it-a-try" since you're probably doing better than they ever saw anyone else do. Your success may excite them. With you as walking proof that this business works, they're more likely to be positive about it. They can continue to focus on your success to give themselves hope. You can, through moving-on yourself in the business, help to silence the naysayers and then little by little, more positive things will be said. Perhaps, in the future, some of them will be sharing what a rough time they gave you in the beginning as part of their success story! That'll sure generate some laughs (and hope), won't it?

Create Your Own Crowd

It's a pretty safe bet to say that most people follow trends, go with the majority, or do whatever seems to be working for "everybody else." So doesn't it make sense to get a "success crowd" together as soon as possible? *You can do nothing and be part of a crowd that's going nowhere. Or you can achieve by helping others – creating your own crowd that makes things happen, with people going toward their goals and dreams.* Where would you rather be?

Each person you help to realize their dreams becomes a part of *your* crowd. As you continue to grow and help more people and they duplicate what you're doing – your crowd grows bigger and stronger. Their understanding of success and their belief in themselves and the credibility of this business also grows stronger in the process. That's why, instead of our success being whispered, the *Wall Street Journal* reports of our strength, high-profile magazines feature our growth, and even television occasionally reports on our positive impact.

The other benefit to this change of public opinion is that it helps strengthen you if you go through a bunch of negative responses. With our credibility growing at a faster rate than ever before, the setbacks along the way no longer have as much of an effect on us as in the past. This is good news – especially for anyone just starting out.

When we keep this in mind as we become more determined than ever, new possibilities emerge. If someone we're approaching for the first time states that they've heard about this before, we'll confidently ask what they've heard.

If they've been misinformed, we'll help them gain a new understanding, that is, if they're open-minded enough to listen. If not, we'll say "NEXT!" and keep going. Or we'll delight in the positive feedback. Either way we win because we're in charge of our attitude – not anybody else! You cannot tailor-make the situations in life, but you can tailor-make the attitudes to fit those situations.

"Others can stop you temporarily – you are the only one who can do it permanently."
Zig Ziglar

E

Chapter Eighteen

Exercise Your Abilities
"Winners never quit and quitters never win."

Stretch Before Any New Workout

Suppose you're just starting to build the business. In the past you may not have been very good at meeting people. You're excited about what you've seen and heard about this opportunity and you believe the time is right for you to go for your dreams. This may be a big change for you. So you want to warm up some to keep your attitude positive as you learn and grow.

After you go through your initial list of prospects, it's important to meet and get to know new people some before you share this business. As the system teaches, build relationships and you can build a solid business. This business, like any other, is built on relationships. Build a friendship and you can build a Directship! Strengthen your relationships, especially those that are weak by sincerely caring about and helping those people. As you follow the system, you'll find the skills you're developing will help you make your strong relationships even stronger.

By simply meeting people with no motive except to expand your base of friends, you will tune-in to the needs of others. You'll notice that they're all on the same channel – WII-FM, "What's In It - For Me?" As you experience personal growth and new relationships develop, you can then find out who's serious about changing their financial picture. You could ask them, *"If you had the chance to substantially increase your income without affecting what you're doing now, would that be of interest to you?"* If so, you can share this business with them with some upline help, if needed.

Do all this at a pace you can handle. Successful people are steady and consistent rather than "biting-off-more-than-they-can-chew." They learn from their mistakes and build their confidence as they go. They keep persisting, even when they're faced with disappointments. They're not whirlwinds who come into the business and go out like a "flash-in-the-pan." They know success takes time. Just like when someone begins a weight training program, trying to lift too much can result in an injured back, with no workouts for a few weeks while they heal. As you exercise your weaker areas, they begin to catch-up with the stronger ones and your progress begins to accelerate. You're building your success on a solid foundation of dynamic relationships with others.

Dangling The Carrot

Generally, people are very good at some part of this business as soon as they start. Some people quickly learn to "show-the-plan" to people they know, but they're just not very good at meeting new people. Others are great at striking up conversations with total strangers but clam up when the opportunity to explain this business comes along. Whatever part of this system appeared easiest to you when you first got "in," was probably what you were already good at.

How can you become good at doing the other things so you're able to build a secure future? Do a lot of what you do well. Set-yourself-up so that you're doing what you already excel at. You can build on your self-confidence in that area as you follow the pattern-of-success.

That sounds great if you're excellent at meeting people because that's where the process starts, right? What if you're a great plan shower? What good is that if you're having difficulty meeting new people?

This business rewards effort that produces positive results. It's an incentive-driven endeavor. Set your mind to that fact and change your perspective. Reward yourself with "showing-the-plan" if that's what you're good at. *Tell yourself that sharing this business is your reward for meeting a certain number of new people each day.* Make what you're good at the reward you give yourself for doing something you're not as confident with. It's a double win. As you "show-the-plan" more often, you're also developing your skills in the area where you're growing more confident. You're "stretching" – building and expanding your skill level as you go. As you keep practicing, you'll get better and better as you fine-tune and add to your skills as you go along. Remember, even though it may seem that way, no one is born knowing how to build this business!

Change Your Mindset – "Ready - Fire - Aim!"

Some people want to wait until they're good at something before they do it. Imagine if you went through life with that attitude. When would you actually take your first step? Say your first word? Ride your first bike? Where would we all be if no one did anything unless they knew ahead of time they'd be good at it?

Expertise is a process in this business just like anything else you do. It involves learning about it, making mistakes doing it, and learning by your mistakes what *not* to do. Through repetition of this process, your confidence grows to the point where you're more comfortable doing what you were afraid to do before. While it doesn't happen overnight, it does occur faster with those who "jump-right-in" and learn and laugh about the lots of mistakes they make until they get the hang of it. They have fun with it! They know they'll never be perfect at it, but they always do the best they can do at that moment in time. They go for excellence – not perfection. Take the attitude of "ready-fire-aim"! Keep "shooting" and adjust your aim as you fire.

Besides, if they were perfect, nobody could relate to them! As you go along and spend more time with the leaders, you'll find out that some of them purposely drop an eraser or make another "mistake," while "showing-the-plan." This is so people can relate to them. It gives others hope that nobody's perfect and that they can goof-up and still succeed!

One of the most important benefits of being in this business is that you're not alone. You can grow in knowledge and experience while having your hand "held" for a while by someone who's been there before. They can help you over the "bumps" while you're learning new things.

You aren't just left to sink or swim, as you would be in many businesses.

When you first get started, that's when your upline people generally want to do some meetings for you. This way you learn how to qualify and invite new people without the pressure of figuring out what to do with them once you've generated interest. You become comfortable with relationship building and prospecting. Then you have someone with experience "show-the-plan" to your prospects. You'll find you'll pick-up on learning the plan pretty quickly even if you need notes in the beginning. It's simple. When you're "showing-the-plan," you can share some things about yourself like upline does. This is part of the relationship building process. Your upline will be happy to teach you what you need to know. Be sure to tape record their plan, as well as other leaders' plans, whenever possible.

While you're still at the early learning stages, with upline's help, you can be bringing people into your business. You'll just keep getting better at meeting new people as you're building your confidence enough to show them this business on your own. Care about the other people and be interested in them – that's the key to your success.

With the system you don't need to spend a lot of time figuring things out for yourself. There are many who've come before you who have made the mistakes. You'll learn what to do and what not to do by listening to your upline. Take advantage of the learning opportunities that the system offers through its training sessions, seminars, rallies, big functions, tapes, and books. Be a good student and you can shorten your learning curve and not repeat the same mistakes. Then you can reach your goals and dreams more quickly. It's worth the effort!

It's The Last One That Does The Most Good

When you're exercising every day and get to the point where you can easily do fifty push-ups, that allows you to maintain your current level of fitness. But suppose you got to fifty, and said to yourself you're going to do five more before you stop. The last five will give you a growth benefit that the first fifty can't. That's because your muscles are accustomed to doing fifty. When you *stretch* them further doing the last five, you cause growth.

You're at a certain point in this business at any given time. If you just got "in," you're at the beginning stage of building your business and reaching for the first pin level. As you follow-the-system, you stretch and see new possibilities which helps you to stay motivated to keep growing. If you've been "in" the business awhile, you may have been at your current level for some time. Perhaps you were comfortable with it before – but now you're ready to make those dreams you've had for so long come true.

You may have reached an age or another point in your life where you realize that if you don't do something now, you'll regret it later. Time's moving-on. Are you? Remember. *No one truly grows old until they let regrets take the place of dreams.*

No matter where you are in the process, you can pick up your pace and make more things happen. For example, say you're now "showing-the-plan twice a week and you motivate yourself to show it three, four, or five times a week. Your business is likely to grow at a faster rate. People who are really on the move, making things happen, may show the plan as much as several times a day! *You grow as you stretch beyond what you're comfortable with.* It's those extra plans you show that can cause more rapid new growth in the size of your group as well as for you in terms of your personal development. Similar to the launching of a rocket, about ninety percent of the fuel is used just getting it off the ground. Once you've "launched" your business and you get momentum, you'll find it's easier to keep going.

As with any exercise, we need to continue to push no matter what level we achieve. Otherwise we can become complacent and begin justifying why we need to do even less. Keep growing even if it's only a tiny fraction each day.

There's no "maintaining" a status quo in the business. You may think you're maintaining but you're not. Remember, time's marching on. Your financial needs are increasing. Inflation continues to eat away at the value of money. If you have children, they're growing and getting more expensive. Maybe they need orthodontic work or they're college bound. Perhaps you have elderly parents who you're supporting. Or you may want to retire soon. All these situations and more are excellent reasons to build this business. The fact is you're either moving ahead or going backward financially. And moving ahead is definitely more exciting! Don't you agree?

"Control your destiny or someone else will. Face reality as it is – not as it was, and not as you wish it were... Change before you're forced to by some outside source."
Jack Welch

R

Chapter Nineteen

Rising To Where You Belong

"When you help others without expecting anything in return, your rewards will be greater than you can imagine."

Winners Don't Keep Score

This business is about helping people achieve their goals and dreams. One thing that holds people back is routinely limiting their assistance. Some set a specific amount of help they're willing to give someone else and then it's payback time. If you have this attitude it'll severely limit your ability to get to where you want to go. (Note that when you counsel with your upline leader and they advise you to shift your attention to other distributors, for whatever reason, that's different. Then there's a good reason to limit your assistance or upline wouldn't suggest you do it.)

Massive growth can occur in your group when help is given with "no-strings-attached." When you help others without expecting anything in return, wonderful things can happen. Your attitude about helping others improves because there's no potential for a disappointing return. This causes you to develop into a sincere giver. It's best to believe in everyone but count on no one (but yourself and your upline that's moving-on).

When you give you'll receive somewhere down the line. Frequently though, what you receive doesn't come from the person you were helping! For example, someone else, who you may not even know, may consider you as an example and want to be a part of your group. They could turn out to be a "shining star" in your organization whose growth fires your other people up! Others may be so inspired by you and the fine leader you are, that they really grab hold of this business and go for it. And since they experience your unconditional service, that's what they duplicate and everyone benefits! The key is to help as many people to be as successful as possible and you'll be appropriately rewarded. As Zig Ziglar says, "You can have everything in life you want, if you will just help enough other people get what they want."

What happens if you set limits? Shutting someone down because they don't respond when and how you'd like them to only slows down the process. If you're expecting to be paid back, and you've decided this is the last time unless they start pulling their weight, what type of attitude do you suppose you'll be projecting?

Forget what this does to other people for a moment. Think about how it affects you. If you have a negative attitude about other people, you become a bit more negative yourself. And that just makes matters worse! When you set giving limits as a condition of your performance, you've set a barrier which will be difficult for you to pass. Maybe if you gave someone just a little more help, they'd have the self-confidence to go Direct. So you need to be careful and counsel with your upline leader when you're thinking of giving up on someone. They'll help you have a positive attitude about the situation and make a quality decision about the right thing to do.

So what can you do if you're tempted to stop giving? What if your new distributor is not listening as well as you'd like? If you're starting to react negatively, stop and ask yourself: "What if I were them? How would I feel?" Do you remember when you first got started? Didn't you want your upline to be patient with you? Were you a little scared? Were you so excited about the business that you tried to learn the system a little too fast and fumbled some? Come on. Be honest. So, be patient. Focus on the person you're helping. Do your best to show them compassion while you're encouraging them to do what they need to do to be successful. Then everybody wins!

"People don't care how much you know until they know how much you care," a wise person once said. Care about those people. People say, "It's easy to love the lovable." Everyone's lovable, believe it or not. It's just that some people are amazingly unskilled in their behavior! Take the challenge to see past a person's difficult behavior to acknowledge the person.

Find the good in them and compliment them on it. Remember, their behavior toward you is a reflection of how they feel about themselves. There's hope for *everyone*. Everyone can develop, when they sincerely want to and do whatever-it-takes.

Do what you can to help them. Don't be attached to the outcome. Hey, they may be another "NEXT!" They may lead you to others. If the only benefit you get out of it is you really learn how to care about people unconditionally – what could that be worth to you down the road?

Learn to believe in people while they're learning to believe in themselves. Show you care about folks and give them some "tough" love along the road of success. This means that you tell them what they *need* to hear (not necessarily what they *want* to hear), in a kind, but firm way. Encourage them to keep going outside their comfort zone. You'll find that, as a result of your giving until it hurts sometimes, you can build a large solid organization. *Keep it as light as you can along the way – have more fun with it! Smile.* Keep things in perspective. You can do it.

Do "Whatever-It-Takes"

When a group of folks gets "into" this business at the same time, there always seems to be someone a bit more enthusiastic than the rest. That person gets a crystal clear vision of where this business can take them and they decide that nothing is going to stop them from their final destination. They realize that when they help a certain number of people get to a certain level, they're free!

Perhaps you've heard others talking. Or maybe it was you who said, "I don't care if I have to put everyone "in" myself to get those people to that level. I'm going for it." Whether you heard it or said it is irrelevant. That concept is key to building this business successfully. Focus on *your* dream. You achieve it by helping others to get to *their* dream. When you do, nothing can stop you.

If people forget this attitude of doing whatever-it-takes, everything seems to go into slow motion. They start making excuses to justify not doing anything. They start rationalizing that they're doing just fine and they don't need the things they put on their dream list. They convince themselves that they're already secure. They start forgetting their reasons for getting involved in the first place.

If you observe yourself or anyone in your group developing such a negative attitude, get yourself or them "plugged-into-the-system." The open meetings, functions, seminars, training sessions, books, and tapes help tremendously to keep your attitude positive and your determination strong. You'll know you're not alone – everyone building the business has many of the same challenges.

When you keep "a serving mind set," your business can grow and become secure. Stay "plugged-into-the-system." *Keep focused on your dreams and help your distributors grow.* This will help you maintain a positive attitude through whatever challenges you need to blast through. With your do "whatever-it-takes," attitude, you'll maintain a level of performance that those in your group can duplicate and teach to their new distributors.

Let Your Reputation Precede You

Becoming known as a servant-leader who'll do whatever-it-takes to help others is essential to building a big business. People are more likely to admire you and want to duplicate you. What if everyone imitated people who served others without thoughts of rewards or payment? The world would be a better place to live, wouldn't it?

On a simpler note, when others can see the rewards you're earning from helping others achieve, they're more likely to follow your lead. You'll give them hope that they can do it too. Perhaps when they understand that you're willing to help them succeed, they will come to you for help with a prospect who intimidates them but who could be a great leader in this business. The confidence you give your distributors, because they know you'll be there for them, can go a long way towards securing your business.

People who are less confident and just starting out can "borrow" some of your confidence and, with your help, can move ahead with their business. (As they follow-the-system, they can grow and become leaders themselves.) Once you have a reputation of being a good server, associating your name with great leadership won't be far behind. Most everyone wants to be associated with greatness and with this business, you are very close to it every day. Build your excellent reputation along with your business and you will see the greatness in your mirror that's been there all along.

Getting There Is More Than Half The Fun

Due to the nature of this business and the principles that it's built on, it's a teamwork effort rather than a lonely endeavor, like some other businesses. To succeed, you need to bring others with you. The more successful you want to be, the more people you need to bring along. How can you not have fun when you're hanging out with a lot of positive-thinking success-oriented people who are moving-on? Especially when you helped them succeed.

With that in mind, accepting a "no" can be a lot easier. When your focus is on where you're going and who's going with you, it not only softens the blow, but more importantly, it keeps things in perspective. "Noes" become part of your journey rather than a big deal. *Grow through the "noes"* so you can bring along as many people as possible who want to go with you. The larger your crowd of "yesses" is, the smaller the affect each "no" will have.

When You Do It, You'll Enjoy The Ride

As you know, doing anything worthwhile takes commitment along with consistent effort and determination. The question is, "Do you want to make all the effort yourself or would you like some help?" My guess is you'd like to have others whose efforts not only lighten the load but also speed the process. They're out there. You just need to find them.

If someone tells you this business doesn't work – they don't understand it, pure and simple. Anything can be accomplished when enough committed people have a vision of its completion, have faith, and pay-the-price by doing whatever-it-takes. *The price of success never changes and it's non-negotiable. You either pay it or you fail.* You can either ante it up by yourself or divide it among those who are committed to making the journey with you.

Let's say that a million dollars is your price tag for success. No matter where the money comes from (as long as it's legal, moral, and ethical), when you get it you're successful. Which do you think is more easily achievable – coming up with the cash yourself, or helping enough people who can contribute what you need?

Help one other person and you only need to pay half. You've reduced what money you personally need to come up with by 50% but $500,000 is still a lot for one person to pay. Help ten people and you only need to personally come up with $100,000. If those ten each helped ten more, the per-person contribution is only $10,000. Still, even that's a bit much for most people.

But what if each of those people helped ten and then helped ten again; then a contribution of $100 from each person would do it! Let's look at the question again. If a million dollars is your admission price for success, would you rather come up with the whole thing or help a lot of people and each of you come up with $100?

I only use dollars as an example. No one is going to pay your admission for you. But, when you help enough others achieve their own levels of success, the residual income that would flow to you would certainly be sizable enough for you to be considered successful.

When you put things into this perspective and consider the bigger picture, individual answers won't have as much of an effect on how you grow. You'll understand that it is the destination that is your objective – not the keeping track of each step along the way. For example, a tennis player's objective is to win the match. They don't count how many times they hit the ball over the net to get there. Whether someone says "yes" or "no," it's really just a step (like a ball over the net). The more steps you take as a student of the system, the faster you can arrive at your destination and the more secure your business can become. It's up to you!

"We conquer by continuing."
George Matheson

Part Three

Staying Power

T

Chapter Twenty

Trying Is Lying

"Nothing was ever accomplished by trying. Things only happen when you do something."

Sometimes Your "Best" Just Isn't Good Enough

You see your goals and dreams ahead of you. When asked if you need help, you may respond that you'd first like to see if you can do it alone. Then you begin analyzing a multitude of outcomes. You envision people laughing at you. You see a basement or garage full of products you don't know what to do with. Lifelong friends are crossing the street to avoid you. You call your upline, tell them you did your "best," but for right now, you're going to slow down.

I know it may sound a little harsh but, in my opinion, it's difficult to slow down if you haven't done anything. You need to control your imagination. Instead of imagining constant doom and gloom, you need to use your imagination to focus on your dreams and goals. Picture *those things* happening. See a basement full of things to make your kids lives better. See a huge crowd of distributors that you helped to be successful coming to your new dream home to thank you. See their cars lining both sides of your street in your new neighborhood!

With those visions in your mind, it would be difficult to tell anyone, including yourself, that you've just done your "best." When you keep your focus on your destination, it becomes difficult for your mind to allow you to make excuses. You're looking for ways to do what you need to do to achieve your goals. You'll begin telling yourself, "Sometimes my 'best' simply isn't good enough. I've just got to get it done; whatever-it-takes." And that's OK! Being successful requires a shift in thinking for most people.

Prove It To Yourself – There's No Such Thing As "Try"

Take a break and go get a pen. Now place it in front of you on a table. Concentrate on it really hard. Imagine the weight of it, the force of gravity pulling down on it, and the effort required to lift it. Focus all of your energy on that pen and in a single movement, *try* to pick it up.

If you tried, you failed. It's *impossible* to *try* to do something. You either picked up the pen or you didn't! You either do it or you don't do it. Those are the only possibilities. Think about it. Picture what *trying* to pick up a pen looks like. Describe it. You can't. There's no way you can demonstrate *trying* to pick up a pen.

Now think about prospecting. Have you been *trying* to prospect? You know, going out to contact new people, hoping they'll want to get "in" your business? Did you imagine that they would approach you and ask if you might have an opportunity that could perhaps change their lives? When no one approaches you under those conditions, do you return home telling yourself that you gave it a *try* but prospecting just doesn't work for you?

Get out there and find some people who will tell you they're not interested! Get some "noes" and learn that those answers won't hurt you. Listen to why they're telling you "no" and perhaps you can fine-tune your approach to increase your odds of success.

There Is Only "Doing"

Many people have a tendency to mentally over-rehearse what they're about to do before they actually go out and do it. Understanding and preparing for what you're going to do is important. However, if you analyze anything "to death" by imagining too many different outcomes, there's a tendency to hesitate or even put off entirely the act of doing it. It's called "paralysis of analysis." Some people just wear themselves out thinking about the business and never actually do it!

To paraphrase an old saying, *"Anything worth doing is worth doing poorly enough times until you get good at it."* When you rehearse potential outcomes in your mind, it's important to picture the outcome you want to create. It's like a self-fulfilling prophesy. *You get what you focus on.* So you need to harness the power of your mind rather than letting it run rampant through a host of negative scenarios.

Your mind is capable of picturing infinite situations, many of which may be outcomes you don't want that can keep playing in front of you. If you don't purposely control it, you can waste a lot of energy worrying about what could happen. You know that you can't possibly anticipate every situation anyway. That would be like saying you could predict the future. Instead calmly tell yourself, "Whatever happens, I can handle it. I'll do my part and whatever the others decide to do is up to them."

When you just go out and do something, there are only a few possible outcomes. Say you go prospecting and someone you approach isn't ready to hear what you have to say. That's not your fault. Or they may think they're ready and tell you it's not for them. That's not your fault, either. It's possible that they don't understand what you've shared with them. You may need to work on how you show-the-plan. Get with your Direct for some pointers.

Then you may find a person who gets excited right away. They may have been hoping for a chance to change their financial picture. So, when you come along and believe in them like no one else ever has, they embrace you and your ideas with open arms. Or you may meet someone who takes a couple of months to decide what they're going to do. They ask to see literature, meet some other people, and go to a seminar before they finally get "in."

The fact is, many people are likely to tell you they're not interested – at least not now. This isn't unique to this business. It happens when people sell insurance, cars, and just about anything else. Ninety-five percent of what you do in this business is preparation for the five percent that'll lead to your success. So it's important to realize and accept this as reality. It'll be easier for you to keep going, doing what you need to do to build your business.

Discover Your Formula

You can be successful in this business. First of all, people want to be associated with others who have a positive attitude. You just need to meet enough people and you'll find some who'll want to do whatever you're doing.

Imagine a parade going down the main street of your town or neighborhood. It stops for a couple of minutes. Now picture yourself asking each person in the parade if they'd like to associate with you. You don't give them any details – they just go by your appearance and personality. Would any of them be interested? The answer is most likely "yes." A few may see you as the type of person they'd enjoy being around, and they'd join you.

Now imagine the same parade stopped and you had a few minutes with each person you spoke to. Would more people join you? They probably would. In the first scene there'd be people who didn't like you from the start and you'd never change their minds. Then there'd be others who were so centered on themselves that they never even heard you. But, there would also be some, who after briefly meeting you, weren't sure what they wanted to do. But given the opportunity to talk to you again in the second scene, they'd be able to make up their minds and join you. And there would be some who liked you immediately, and without hesitation they said, "Yes."

This is emotional arithmetic. When you "show-the-plan" to enough people, some will get "in" almost instantly, while others will refuse just as fast. Some will wait and decide that this opportunity isn't for them, while others will come to a bigger meeting for more information before saying "no." Some will only need a little information and they're excited enough to get "in." Others may need to explore all aspects of the business by going to seminars and meeting as many successful people as they can before they go for it. You can figure this out like a *formula* that's tailor made for you.

Let's say that for every person you invite who actually shows up for an opportunity meeting, you need to speak to ten. Say for every person who gets into your business, you need three to attend a meeting. Simply put, you need to talk to thirty people to put one in your business. This number is just an example and your experience may be different, but just imagine what the possibilities can be! *You need to "go-through-the-numbers," as impersonal as it may sound, because doing that and fine-tuning your skills is what works.*

Once you discover your own "prospecting-to-sponsoring" numbers, you no longer need to be discouraged about your growth or the individual answers you may get along the way. In the above example, when you contact one person a day you will sponsor one person a month! Contact more; sponsor more. The prospects answers aren't as important as they once seemed; you've reduced them to a simple formula. As you meet more people, you'll also get better with the process. Chances are, your formula will improve and you'll sponsor even more.

The important thing with this formula is that once you've discovered yours, the thinking is over and things will probably get better. There is no longer a need to rehearse this in your mind. You know what you're dealing with. You no longer just *try* to sponsor people. You choose to either *do it* or not, based on how serious you are about achieving your goals and dreams. What do you *really, really, really* want? Do you see that you can have what you want through building this business? Are you going to *"go-for-it"* and *"make-it-happen"*?

> *"When we give it our all, we can live with ourselves —*
> *regardless of the outcome."*

O

Chapter Twenty-One

Open Your Heart –
Your Mind Will Follow

"Success is due less to ability than to zeal."
Charles Buxton

Perfect Sense?

You've seen the numbers, the annual sales, the forty year track record, the millions of people involved. This business concept and the methods used make perfect sense. It's an excellent example of Free Enterprise. Every type of media now praises its success as a proven method of building a secure financial future. Why then will some of the people you approach tell you this "thing" will never work? Why do some still think it's illegal? Or a scam?

Ultimately, many of these people know that this business works. The doubt they have is often in themselves and in their ability to be successful. They cover up their fear by saying this business isn't for them. They might add that they don't know anyone who'd be interested in something like this. Or, they knew a friend of a friend's second cousin's brother-in-law's daughter's teacher who got stuck with a basement full of stuff and lost everything. (I've followed up on some of these stories and not one of them proved to be true. They were just rumors.) The fact is some people will go to any length to come up with an excuse (a thin shell of truth stuffed with a lie) to avoid facing their fears and doing it anyway.

When you've done all you can to help somebody understand the potential and they still don't want to get "in," do yourself a favor and move-on. Don't even attempt to disprove rumor and innuendo. It's not worth it. That's usually not what's keeping them from getting "in." They probably felt they had to come up with something negative to justify their refusal. And maybe they didn't have enough courage to just say "no."

The truth is, no matter what their reasons or excuses may be, everyone has the right to make their own choices. They then get to live with the results of those decisions like all of us do. *The quality of your life is based largely on the quality of your choices.*

Don't Even Think About It

You've already seen the financial mathematics of this business. Taking out all the elements of the business – the system, the people, the products and services, and the income, all you're left with are the numbers. Just understanding it from that perspective, without any other information, it makes perfect sense. You can mathematically prove this business works.

While that may be important to know, it's not the main reason people get "in." *People in a free society usually act on emotion.* They often purchase things based on how they make themselves feel (by their thoughts about it) when they anticipate owning it. Otherwise we would have cars that were all the same size and color rather than a variety of choices for different preferences. Emotion is why one person would rather buy a hot sports car while his or her neighbor dreams of owning a fully-equipped pickup truck.

When you stop analyzing *how* the business works and start using this vehicle to achieve your *why*, you'll increase your chances of attracting like-minded people who'll be receptive and say "yes." The other benefit is that those who do say "no" will have little effect on you because you know *why* you're doing this. You're moving ahead, regardless of what anyone else does. Know your *why* and always keep it in front of you. Drive toward your dream.

Think about what you're currently doing for work. Whether you're employed or in your own business doesn't matter for this example. What if I asked you this: Could I automatically be successful in your business if you told me *how* to do it? Probably not, right? But what if I had a dream, and saw your business as my ticket to make it come true? Then I'd have a better chance of succeeding, even if I don't have all the knowledge, right? Well, the same is true about being successful in general – you "gotta" have a *dream,* a *why!*

Excitement Involves

Have you ever been to a fireworks display? Probably. Did you enjoy it? Most people do. The colors, noise, and cheers from the crowd help get you caught up in the moment. You can't help but feel the excitement. Your senses are heightened and you enjoy the feeling you have when each rocket climbs and bursts into brilliance in the sky. Aren't all these the reasons why you go? If you have children, don't you bring them along so they can experience the same feelings?

Have you ever toured a fireworks factory? Probably not. It's likely most of you aren't interested in how all the rockets and flares are made – you're just interested in enjoying the end result.

This business is similar. To get started people only need a very basic understanding of how this business actually works. (They might think they need all the details, depending on their personality, but they don't.) To be successful, though, they need to have a *passion* for achieving their dreams. And because of your excitement, they believe you'll be there to help and encourage them to get where they want to go.

Still don't get it? Next time you're at a party, ask someone to show you how they figured out their taxes this year. Have them show you, calculation-by-calculation, until you're either asleep or they've finished. Is there anything less stimulating to most people than discussing how to figure out taxes? But, ask a crowd at the same party to describe their *feelings* about taxes and you'd better put on the coffee. You could be there for days, listening to this emotionally-charged issue!

One question dealt with logic and the other with emotion. When you attract people, which one of those elements is the draw? Emotion, again. If it works on issues, why wouldn't it work in business? The answer is it can. And it does! That's why seminars and functions are focused more on the *why* behind this business than on the *how*. When you're excited about your *why,* you can help others be excited too. Then they'll be more open to learning the *how.*

Lead Them With Your Heart

One of the teachings of the business is, as I mentioned before, *"People don't care how much you know until they know how much you care – about them."* This means that completely understanding all bonus levels and other details of this business, will only help you grow when you care about and help other people to win. When you start helping and caring about your prospects and those who get "in" with you, you can grow at a much faster rate. In line with this is your general concern for people and how you show it to upline and others you associate with.

If you simply manage your organization, rather than lead them, it becomes a pile of boring statistics. You'll begin dictating how many plans "must" be shown by your group for you to grow. The problem is, most people already have a job and all the negative trappings associated with it. They don't need or want you to create another one. One boss is more than enough for most.

By getting excited over each person's accomplishments, no matter how small they may seem, you can create an emotional bond within your group. Those who aren't currently doing much in the business may notice you responding to those who are consistently doing little things to grow and perhaps they'll want to be part of that. Maybe it'll give them the incentive to do some more prospecting. Or, they may do one more follow-up just to get some of your recognition. While there may be no logic in this, it's what makes a people business flourish. People like to be appreciated and recognized as valuable contributors.

Logic can be managed while emotions need to be led. Managing tends to contain while leading encourages growth. Thinking too much can cause paralysis of analysis and slow growth. Your emotions of excitement and caring about others can cause people to follow and duplicate your efforts. Would you like faster growth? Put your heart into it!

What do I mean when I say, "Lead them with your heart"? First of all, *people don't really hear you unless you're speaking from your heart.* Have you ever noticed that you're most moved when a speaker sincerely communicates from their heart? They may get very passionate about the parts of their talk that are most dear to them. Their voice may crack a little; tears may well up in their eyes; or they may stop for a moment and you can feel the audience responding emotionally.

I'm not saying that you need to jump up and down or cry to communicate. But you do need to be genuine and spontaneous. And you know what else? You need to be filled with love. Some of you, who for years have associated leadership with logical process and authority, may think love is only meant for families and close friends. At the risk of sounding corny, *love is essential for leadership.* I don't mean you always need to be showing affection or falling all over people in an *attempt* to be loving. That's "trying" to love by going through the motions. It does mean you need to be somewhat vulnerable, though.

Love is necessary in excellent leadership, or if you feel more comfortable with the word "care," that's OK too. The need for caring is universal in all types of organizations, not just this business. To honestly take your eyes off yourself and care about people is the banner of a true leader. A leader who respects and cares about others can create a *sense of community* (of which caring is the basis) in his or her organization. Community is composed of people who are bonded by their sense of compassion. It's not done "at the drop of a hat." No, it takes time and the development of mutual trust. Such a leader brings out the best in people. They honor people and recognize them as unique individuals with something to give to the organization as a whole. Do you honestly want to be a strong leader? Lead them with your heart!

> *"For the resolute and determined there is time and opportunity."*
> Ralph Waldo Emerson

Part Four

Success

Y

Chapter Twenty-Two

You're This Close To Greatness

*"Everyone has it within his power to say, this I am today,
that I shall be tomorrow."*
Louis L'Amour

It's Where You're Going That Matters

Have you ever been driving at night on the highway and gone right past your exit? You were so busy thinking about something else or watching the road and traffic, that you forgot to look for the exit sign. If you were fortunate, you realized what happened and turned around at the next exit. However, you may have been so engrossed in everything else around you that you drove many miles before you realized you went way past your destination exit.

When you always keep your dreams and goals in front of you, you'll be excited as you take each step and get closer and closer to where you want to be. You'll realize, as you achieve each goal, that you're better able to make out the details of your destination as they come into clearer focus. The little bumps and detours along the way don't even matter – they're just part of your journey.

Another benefit to focusing on your dreams (destination) is it's easier to reset your goals, if necessary, along the way. You won't be so concerned if it takes you longer than what you expected to make your dreams come true. You know your destination is more important than how long it takes to get there. And you're sure you'll make it; you're just not sure when. I don't know any successful millionaires who are asked how long it took them to become wealthy. They arrived and the time it took doesn't matter. Besides, most success is measured in steps – not time. If you wait between steps, it takes longer. However, when you step quickly, you'll almost certainly arrive at your destination sooner.

The Past Does Not Equal The Future

Shortly after you started in this business, you probably made some decisions. It's likely you told yourself that you wanted to reach a certain level. You may have set personal, financial, and other goals for yourself so you could make those dreams come true.

You need to fully understand that whatever obstacles you've encountered since you first got "in," in and of themselves, have little to do with your ability to accomplish these goals and dreams. Regardless of the failures and setbacks you may have endured, your success is just as achievable as anyone else's. Yesterday's gone but you have a clean slate with each new day – a new beginning.

Unsuccessful people decide how many times they'll "show-the-plan" this week, based on the responses of last week. Successful people, regardless of how many "noes" they got last week, "show-the-plan" just as often, or more, as they did last week, depending on how quickly they want to reach their goals. The people who said "no" last week won't have any effect on your business this week – unless you let them. The only power they have over you is the power you give them to stop you from going on toward your destination. (The truth is, they probably aren't interested in stopping you at all – they've just made a decision about *themselves!*)

Let's say you set a goal of helping three people reach their own level of independence, which may be different for each of them – depending on their financial situation. Before you start on that journey, ask yourself this question, "Is there any one person who is key to my success?" Yes – you! *There's no other single individual other than you who'll cause you to succeed or fail.* Again, believe in everyone, but count on no one but yourself and your moving-on upline!

What possible difference can a few negative responses make? For that matter, what difference could one thousand negative responses make? Of course they can make a positive difference when you accept each one as a learning experience. However, the only negative difference they can make is if you let them.

When you stay focused on your dream, concentrating on reaching each goal to your destination as you help others, nothing that occurs in the past can affect you. Remember, as soon as someone gives you their answer, it's history. *If it's a "no" you say "NEXT!"* Learn everything you can from the experience, and keep on moving. When it's a "yes," "plug-them-into-the-system" as you help them and keep on driving toward your next goal. It's as simple as that.

How Will You Know Unless...?

The next three people you speak to could be *the ones* who get "in" and build a big business. How will you know what they're going to do unless you talk to them? They may be attracted to you because they sense your positive attitude and are looking for an opportunity to change their lives. They could have all the leadership skills and desire to succeed that you've been looking for. But if you let last week's "noes" cloud your thinking, you may never even notice. So let go of these "noes" and clear your vision so you can see the possibilities before you!

Say you happen to meet someone who's having a tough time "making ends meet" (having enough money to pay all their bills), but they haven't given up on themselves. They might be excited about the business and the fact that you can help them get the security and freedom they want. Of course, they may also turn you down just like the last few people you spoke to did. You could always wonder what may have happened had you shared the business with them and let that bother you. Or, you can be sure one way or the other about whether they'd be interested. How could you possibly know until you ask? Even if they say "no" now, they may change their mind and get "in" later.

You have tremendous possibilities with this business. And there's only one way to definitely sort them out. *You must press on!* Whether that means approaching the "NEXT!" person, attending the "NEXT!" meeting, ordering the "NEXT!" business building tools, or counseling with your upline leader, you need to keep going. For your own piece of mind, you owe it to yourself to explore all the possibilities. And how can you be sure whether somebody's interested or not, unless you ask? How will you know what you can do with this business if you don't give it your all?

The Excitement Of Possibility

Focusing on the potential positive outcome of doing something can often excite you enough to go do it. This improvement in your attitude can actually affect that outcome. Your positive expectation can be a self-fulfilling prophesy. Look for the good though, no matter what happens. (In some cases, a positive outcome may be that you learned a lot from that experience.) As I stated earlier, people are often attracted to those who exhibit a positive attitude. When you're excited about the possibilities, rather than overwhelmed by the potential negatives, that shows in your appearance and behavior towards others. You become an attraction rather than a distraction!

Your excited, positive attitude can grow stronger and you'll have even more confidence. Your enthusiasm can fire up your prospects too. Or, at least you won't let their questions rattle you or throw you off-track. If they say "no," you won't let it slow you down at all. *Each time you share the business with someone, you're taking one step closer to your own success.* It's important to note that I didn't mention whether this person got "in" or not. What's important is that you're taking the steps to share this business opportunity with them. And you're doing that as many times as it takes to reach your dreams and goals.

If I lose sight of my dreams for a moment or start to doubt myself, I pick up one of my favorite books. I go to the page that I've permanently marked and read it. I'd like to share it with you.

"...I will persist until I succeed.

I was not delivered into this world in defeat, nor does failure course in my veins. I am not a sheep waiting to be prodded by my shepherd. I am a lion and I refuse to talk, to walk, to sleep with sheep. I will hear not those who weep and complain, for their disease is contagious. Let them join the sheep. The slaughterhouse of failure is not my destiny.

I will persist until I succeed.

The prizes of life are at the end of each journey, not near the beginning; and it is not given to me to know how many steps are necessary in order to reach my goal. Failure I may still encounter at the thousandth step, yet success hides behind the next bend in the road. Never will I know how close it lies unless I turn the corner.

Always will I take another step. If this is of no avail I will take another, and yet another. In truth, one step at a time is not too difficult...."

Og Mandino, *The Greatest Salesman in the World*

E

Chapter Twenty-Three

Everybody Has A Story

"You have no idea how big the other fellow's troubles are."
B.C. Forbes

Who Would You Approach?

In order to be efficient you may figure you need to eliminate those "who couldn't possibly use this business." You know who I mean – those people "who'll say 'no' because they've already achieved their dreams." You may think that by avoiding these people you won't be subjecting yourself to a bunch of definite "noes," since you're likely to get plenty anyway.

Should lawyers be on your list? Some of them are high-profile, high-success businesspeople who get the big bucks settling big cases. These folks have it made. So what if they work 75-90 hours per week? Most have six-figure student loans and other start-up debt. Their average income falls right in line with the national average even when they're just getting started. They may enjoy the tremendous stress and pressure they're under every day. But then again, maybe they don't.... Let's leave them on the list. The truth is, a recent poll of lawyers shows that 70 percent of them would like to get out of the law field.

What about stockbrokers? Many people (especially in the United States) know of the Wall Street Stock Exchange in New York. Isn't there a lot of money and power there? Aren't they all under 30 years old and millionaires? Or are they? Surely they don't need another business, do they? For all those who rose to the top quickly and have the portfolio to match, there are also hundreds who lost it all in a matter of hours. Hmm.... Perhaps they might be interested in a residual income that keeps coming in, regardless of what happens to the rest of their money. Let's put them on the list.

How about doctors? Aren't they the richest people in town – especially surgeons? They're absolutely all set. Or are they? Golf every Wednesday. Vacation homes. Short hours. They *probably* can absorb the decrease in income that insurance and health reform have brought. That's all because the insurance companies, in order to keep premiums down to customers, are paying doctors less per patient while the reforms in health care are limiting the choices people have as to which doctor they may choose. But, the decrease in patients who are forced to see other doctors probably hasn't affected them. The cost of insurance against malpractice isn't increasing all that fast. Perhaps some doctors would like to be in a position where they could practice medicine the way they want to rather than hustling around for patients to keep the doors open. Nope. Better not cross them off the list. (The truth is, most doctors work 60 to 100 hours a week and have virtually no time for a life!)

Everyone you know and meet who's serious about their future is entitled to an opportunity to be shown the plan and hear *your* story. When you keep this in mind, you can really begin to share the heart of this business. You ask about what your prospects want – "What are your dreams?" You share the potential of this business and how it can help them make their dreams come true. You reach down into your heart and share what this business means to you – the fine people you're associating with, the fun you're having, the changes you're experiencing in your life – whatever is true for you. You duplicate what your upline leaders are teaching you about "showing-the-plan." You do the best you can, using notes if you need to.

Then it's up to your prospects. It's their decision whether or not they want to learn more, because it's their life isn't it? It's not right to decide whether they want what this business offers or not. Care about them and be other-centered. You're not attached to anybody getting "in." You know that your people are out there and you can find them, when you are committed and doing "whatever-it-takes." Don't count anybody out or "in," for that matter, before they've shared their questions, concerns, and level of interest. Even at that point, they can change their mind. So, listening and being flexible and understanding is key. Use the "Platinum Rule" – "Do unto others as they would have you do unto them" (Treat others as they want to be treated).

Shifting The Burden Of Proof

For many years we have been compiling evidence to prove to people that this business really works. The "trial" is over. There is absolutely no way for anyone to show that this opportunity doesn't represent one of the greatest potentials for income and security in the world. We have more than enough proof.

Whether it's individuals who have become millionaires (there are hundreds of them), magazines who sing praises and point out successes, the awards received (from presidents and even the United Nations), or just the thousands of people whose lives have changed for the better, this business has worked for nearly four decades.

Each time you're sharing the business with someone, keep that in mind. Perhaps you might try shifting the burden of proof on them. Perhaps you can ask them to share with you what they've done to put themselves in a position where they truly don't need this. After all, you can tell them that you're a businessperson and, as such, you're open-minded and always looking for other ways to diversify your income. If there's anything better out there, you sure want to learn about it. And besides, you can tell them, when you get to a certain level in this business, you'll be looking for something to do during the day. You won't need your current job or business anymore and may decide to retire. Maybe they believe there's another way out there to create residual income that works better than this business does. Maybe the next person you talk to knows what it is. Ask them to tell you about it! You're likely to find that they suddenly become speechless!

Music To Your Ears

Whether you're just starting out or you've been building your business for years, one thing is certain. You know more about the business than most prospects you talk to. Be aware that there are insecure people out there who are intimidated by those who have more knowledge on a subject than they have. They can become defensive and attack many of the things you stand for. If you respond defensively, you'll just alienate them, possibly forever. That's a lose-lose situation. That's not what this business is about.

We're about caring about others – no matter how unskillful their behavior is. The more difficult they are to deal with, the more likely they're hurting because their life isn't working (which is no small wonder). This conflict doesn't "do anybody any good." They become so entrenched in their position that they couldn't listen to you, even if part of them wanted to.

There's a simple and relatively easy way to avoid this situation which could even increase your success rate when prospecting. Let them tell you *their* story. Just like any relationship, both sides need to get to know each other. Since you already know yourself and where you're heading, why not let this person begin by telling you more about themselves? Especially if they're a new acquaintance, how can you hope to help them if you don't know much about them?

I once met someone who had all the signs of a great prospect. I approached him and introduced myself. Fortunately, I was already in the habit of allowing the other person to talk first. What I found out about them was that they were having huge personal problems. Adding a business concept to the mix at that time would have been futile.

However, since I took the time to listen, we stayed in touch. When he had resolved his situation, I complimented him on his strength to see it through and told him that he's exactly the kind of person I enjoy working with. We continued talking periodically and today that person is "in" my group. It took almost a year from the initial contact to the day he got "in. However, if I had sprung the plan on him when we first met, he would probably have been lost forever. Timing is key in building this or any other business.

Making People Investments

Investments are something we make today without expecting a payout tomorrow. When you invest, you're in it for the long haul. Like other businesses, this business too has "investments" and "windfalls." Both are equally important and you need to pay attention to both for maximum results. Having both brings more stability to your income and long-term growth. If you try to specialize in one, you may fail at both.

"Windfalls" in this business, are people who, due to whatever's happening in their life, are "sick-and-tired-of-being-sick-and-tired" and are seriously looking to do something to improve their situation. When you discover such a person, and sponsor them into the business, they often take off like a rocket and begin growing right away. Their desire is so strong that they let nothing stand in their way. They see this opportunity as exactly what they've been looking for and will "ride it" for all it's worth.

A people "investment" is a long-term, big-pay, work-in-progress. They may get "in" initially and take baby steps, while learning all they can. They may not have had a specific desire when you first met, but got "in" based on your integrity and enthusiasm. You need to nurture a dream in them. Once they have it, they will begin to grow. Such people start slow and pick up momentum.

They may also be like the person I described earlier, who in many ways was ideal for this business, but due to personal difficulties, the initial timing wasn't right. They may even have said "no" to the opportunity before, but left the door open in case something changed. These are the people you build a long-term caring relationship with before they build the business. They're the seeds you plant that sprout later. The benefit to having these people in your group is that they're often your most loyal supporters. They know you care about them and they grow to care about you, too.

You Have Two Ears And One Mouth

Did you know that, in most cases, people enjoy talking about themselves more than anything? And they like hearing other people say nice things about them too! Not too surprising, is it? Keeping this in mind will help you a great deal, especially when you meet somebody for the first time. In fact, I have an opening line that may help you determine if you're speaking to a windfall or an investment. You can then focus your energies for the greatest result.

You: Hello. My name is _____ and you are?
Prospect: Tom. How's it going?
You: Real good. How about you?

At this point subjects like work and family begin to enter the conversation. You can then use what's called "the elevator speech." The elevator speech is describing what you do in the time it takes an elevator to pick you up at one floor and drop you off at the next. Here's how it goes:

You: You know how a lot of people don't seem to have enough time and money? What I do is help them develop ways of leveraging themselves to the point where they have plenty of both.

There are only three possible responses to this statement. **One reaction is** that they aren't listening, so they ignore you and go on talking about themselves. This is "OK" – it gives you some insight about that person. (Remember, just observe, rather than judge.) It also shows them what a good listener you are. You may hear something you can use later – which is called "free information."

The second response they may give you is a question. "How do you do that?" Your response here is critical. Don't explain it just yet. You say, "Tell me about your situation and I'll see if I can apply what I do to you." You're demonstrating a willingness to help the person you've just met. This can create quite a favorable situation. Listen to their response and "take them where they want to go."

The third response is one you may not anticipate if you assume the only outcomes are going to be a "yes" and a "no." So it's important to be open to the possibility that they'll say, "Hey, I know somebody who could use that." You may well increase the number of referrals you receive when you do your elevator speech!

After you make your statement about the leveraging you teach people to do, let the person you're talking to tell you *their* story or possibly give you a referral.

"Listening involves patience, openness, and the desire to understand – highly developed qualities of character."
Stephen R. Covey

S

Chapter Twenty-Four

Start Starting

"Beginning is half done."
Robert H. Schuller

Only Two Possibilities

Congratulations! You're in the homestretch. These last few pages will hopefully tie things up and help you get going. For those of you who read things that you've been doing all along, you can be more confident that you're on the right track.

For this information to be useful you need to *do something* with it. Action is key. You need to get out there and use what you've learned and keep track of the results. If you just sit there and don't share this business with anybody else, only you will know about it and others you know or meet who *could* benefit probably never will. You may be the only one who would ever approach them about this business.

You need to talk with those people who you've been putting off talking to. You also need to meet new people who are serious about changing their financial picture. Listen to their story to determine what they want, share what you know, take a look at your results, and determine how much closer you're getting to your goals and dreams. Then decide. Decide what? Decide what you can do "NEXT!" Fine-tune your skills, get more fired up, go through your "noes" faster, or what? What will help you move-on more quickly? When you've *been there and done that* – then, as a leader, you can speak confidently about what you've learned along the line. Your story can be an inspiration to others.

Put this question on a sheet of paper or card and post it where you'll see it often:

What am I doing today to be a _____ *?*
(Write in your desired level of accomplishment, e.g. Diamond.)

"CANI"

Over the years I've come to appreciate the acronym **CANI** – **C**onstant **A**nd **N**ever-ending **I**mprovement. The people building this business base much of their success on this philosophy. You too can participate in the constant improvement of your ability to build this business. Use what you've learned in this book and from other resources in the system. Use your knowledge until you're so comfortable with it that it's almost second nature. When that occurs, ask yourself this question, "What can I do to make it even better?"

When you're truly comfortable with this information, you'll know what to do "NEXT!" Your new understanding will take these ideas and your business to the next level.

Those constant little improvements, along with caring about other people, are what has made this business and the leaders in it so great. And there's still unlimited growth potential. There's plenty of room for you to shine and make those cherished dreams and goals a reality.

The Diamond And The Dirt

A piece of coal doesn't become a diamond overnight. It takes years of heat and pressure before it turns into a precious gem. You and your business are the same way.

If you were to lay a piece of coal (a new idea) on the ground, how many years would it take to become a diamond? It never will. But if you're serious about having the diamond how could you be sure it will change?

That piece of coal will never amount to anything more unless you place some pressure on it. Too much pressure too soon and you'll crush it. Place a shovel full of dirt on it (a slight improvement) and not much will happen. Continue to add a shovel at regular intervals, getting help from others who have the same goals and dreams. Before long that piece of coal will be sitting under a mountain of improvements (the positive pressure of success) and will begin its transformation. As certain as the sun rises, in time and under enough pressure, it will become a diamond.

What you need to realize is you cannot create that mountain of improvement in one day. When you wake up tomorrow, there won't automatically be a diamond at your door. But, when you pick up your shovel and go after your dream a shovel-full at a time, never giving up, you can enjoy the life you have dreamed of living. Each day brings you closer to the reality you want to create. What happened yesterday is of little consequence compared to what you do today...and each day, until you make your dreams come true.

Remember – *"SW, SW, SW – 'NEXT!'"*

By now, you have an appreciation for the *attitude* you need to build a big business. Who knows how many people you'll need to meet and share the opportunity with, in order to succeed? Whatever that number may be, always remember that you're in the duplication business. Set a good example for others to follow and help *them* develop *the "NEXT!" attitude.* And, regardless of your prospects' responses, just *"keep-going-through-the-numbers."*

There are those along-the-line who will want to get "in" and build the business. For them you'll say, *"Some Will – 'NEXT!'"* and you'll keep sharing the business with others, not resting on your "laurels." Others "won't-see-the-forest-for-the-trees" and wouldn't get "in" even if you did all the work for them! Just say, *"Some Won't – 'NEXT!'"* Regardless of what they decide, stay focused on *your* dream. Don't be concerned with the answers you get along the way. Just say, *"So What – 'NEXT!'"* Just keep saying – *"Some Will, Some Won't, So What – 'NEXT!'"*

This doesn't mean you don't care about other people. But you have a mission – you're looking for people who want a better life and will work to get it. Remember the old cliché, *"You can lead a horse to water, but you can't make him drink." The "NEXT!"* attitude simply means you're not going to let *their* decisions determine *your* future. *You're* in control of your life and *nothing's* going to stop you from making your dreams come true – certainly not any "noes" you get. *"If they say 'no,' just say – 'NEXT!'"*

I hope the information I've shared with you in this book helps you reach new heights in the business. I also hope it helps you maintain your compassion for others, while at the same time, not letting other people's decisions affect your determination. *You can do it, you know – you really can!*

About the Author

John Fuhrman is first and foremost a husband and father. He is also a speaker, peak performance trainer, and consultant. He is founder and president of Frame of Mind, Inc., an organization dedicated to the motivation and performance enhancement of all clients. He has been an award-winning sales producer and manager and entrepreneur. He is a current member of the National Speakers Association, and has been featured in *Selling Magazine* as an authority on rejection.

Through large doses of personal experience, coupled with humor, John has helped enhance the performance of sales and business professionals throughout the world. He is a sought-after speaker and author on success, motivation, management, and team building, as well as leadership and networking.

For more information on seminars and other training programs or to see if John's programs can fit into your next function, contact Frame of Mind, Inc., 89 Bayberry Lane, Manchester, NH 03104; phone (888)883-3303; fax (603)622-3859; e-mail rejectme@aol.com; or visit John on the Internet at www.expertspeak.com.

John lives with his wife, Helen, and their two children, John and Katie.